HOW TO PU

COFFEE TABLE BOOK

HOW TO PUBLISH A

COFFEE TABLE BOOK

*The essential guide to taking your book
from idea to publication*

TAPIWA MATSINDE

First published in the United Kingdom in 2022 by Shoko Press

How to Publish a Coffee Table Book © 2022
Tapiwa Matsinde

All Rights Reserved.

British Library Cataloguing-in-Publication Data
A catalogue record for this book is available from the British Library

ISBN 978-0-9954706-8-2

For those brave enough to see where their dreams will lead.

About the Author

Tapiwa Matsinde is an author, storyteller, curator, mentor, and blogger. She has published several books using the traditional publishing and self-publishing routes. Tapiwa's award-winning blog *atelier 55* formed the basis of her debut illustrative book *Contemporary Design Africa*. Based on her experiences Tapiwa has written *How to Publish a Coffee Table Book* as a guide to help other content creators, professionals, entrepreneurs, and writers who want to publish their own coffee table books. She lives in London, UK.

Contents

Part One: Preparing Yourself for the Process of Publishing a Coffee Table Book

Part Two: Planning Your Coffee Table Book

Part Three: The Publishing Process, What to Expect

Part Four: Promotion

Resources

A Coffee Table Book: a definition

The term 'coffee table book', used throughout this publication,
collectively refers to books whose subject matter is usually non-
fiction lifestyle, such as photography, interiors, fashion, cooking,
beauty, art, design, architecture, and so forth.

Other names for coffee table books are illustrative books, artbooks,
cocktail books or lifestyle books. More than decorative props, coffee
table books have served to document contemporary culture, delving
into subjects ranging from portraits by celebrity photographers, to
behind-the-scenes looks into couture fashion houses, to travelogues
of places that most people can only dream about, adding to the coffee
table book's desirability.

Author's Note

Hi, my name is Tapiwa. In January 2013, at the start of a brand new year, I had been blogging for two years and two months and was looking at ways to monetize my blog and become more visible in my industry. A book was one option that interested me. Inspired by fellow bloggers who were publishing books, I took a leap of faith and began the process of writing and producing my own. Later that year, in December 2013 to be exact, I landed and signed a traditional publishing deal with a leading artbook publisher to write my first book, *Contemporary Design Africa*. Then, in 2016, I self-published my second book, *Fashion Illustration Africa*.

The idea of writing a book had always been lurking in the deep recesses of my mind, but I never really thought it was possible until I began writing my blog. I knew nothing about the publishing industry and did not have a journalistic background in the traditional sense, so I found myself learning the ropes as I went along (something I suspect many of you reading this have found yourselves doing too). Now, having been through a challenging, yet highly rewarding process, I am sharing my experiences and tips in this straightforward, practical guide to creating and publishing a coffee table book to help those of you who are looking to do the same. It's the kind of guide I wish I'd had when I started.

I should point out that this is not a book about how to write a coffee table book, but rather a guide to the process of creating and publishing one. Whilst the information contained in this book focuses on content creators, whom I categorize as bloggers, social media platform owners, video content producers, podcasters, writers, artists, and photographers, amongst others; it applies equally to anyone in any number of industries who wants to produce a coffee table book. Remember, everyone's journey is different, so what worked for me may not necessarily work for you, but I am confident you will find the information useful in getting you on your way.

Tapiwa Matsinde

Introduction

So, you have been creating content for a while and are now thinking you might turn your hand to print or, at the very least, a more comprehensive digital publication. But where to start and what to do?

No matter where in the world you are, publishing a coffee table book has never been easier. The relative ease of self-publishing has empowered people from all walks of life to bring their stories and individual perspectives to print and digital formats.

Blogging gave birth to the content creator, which, in turn, paved the way for the creation of some inspiring, diverse and original books that might otherwise never have seen the light of day. And you do not need to have a popular or influential blog, social media platform, video channel or podcast read, viewed or listened to by millions each month to produce a coffee table book. My blog was certainly nowhere near as widely read as that, and outside of my niche I am a relatively unknown content creator. What I had, though, was conviction about my subject. I spotted a gap in the market for deeper information on my niche, was clear about my objective, and could communicate this. Thankfully, my publisher agreed.

Some content creators are fortunate enough (depending on your view) to have a publisher approach them first. The rest of us, however, need to take matters into our own hands and either self-publish or contact publishers directly with a proposal for our idea. I did the latter after realizing that, if I wanted to publish an artbook, daydreaming about a publisher contacting me with a deal was likely to get me nowhere. I needed to get in front of them and show why my niche was important and why my blog was worthy of becoming a book.

I also explored the alternative publishing options that were available to me should I fail to secure a publishing deal, or choose not to accept the contract offered.

Taking the initiative calls for a lot of self-belief, along with a [healthy] dose of realistic expectations to balance things out, but one thing I was certain about was that blogging had allowed me to hone my writing and research skills, and deepened my knowledge of my industry. In the process, this had boosted my self-confidence to tackle a much larger project, such as publishing a book. I was more than ready, or so I thought...

I underestimated just how challenging putting a book together and the whole publishing process would be, even with a publisher guiding the way. So before you embark on the journey, you do need to ask yourself if it is truly something you can do and want to commit to.

PART ONE:

Preparing Yourself for the Process of Publishing a Coffee Table Book

Creating and publishing a coffee table book takes a high level of focus and commitment. This is especially true if you are self-publishing, as you will be taking on most, if not all, the roles that are normally undertaken by a traditional publisher.

In this section, we will look at preparing yourself for the task ahead and examine:

- The reasons why you want to turn your content into a book and the reasons why you should not

- Managing your expectations

- Getting yourself into the right frame of mind

- Being realistic with the time that you can dedicate to the task

Having clarity in these areas will serve to increase your chances of a) starting it, and b) completing it.

So...

Why Turn Your Content into a Coffee Table Book?

This is an important question that every author or would-be author should ask themselves before putting pen to paper or tapping the keyboard. Knowing why you want to turn your content into a book will help you make the decisions that follow.

There are many reasons why you may want to turn your content into a coffee table book, the most obvious being to set yourself up as an expert in your field. All too often, I find that I get dismissed as being 'just another blogger' when I mention that I am a blogger or content creator. I am not taken seriously and there is still unspoken skepticism about it being a real job. But when I mention that I am an author, the conversation shifts and the level of respect increases. Also, in an increasingly content noisy world, a book can help you, your platform or business, if this is your goal, to stand out from the crowd and increase your credibility.

Other reasons for turning your content into a book include:

- Turning your hard work into a tangible record of your online efforts, especially if you no longer want to keep creating content, for whatever reason

- Making your work available to offline audiences

- Helping you to attract a new audience demographic

- Creating more detailed content to complement what you have already. This gives you a chance to expand on topics and themes that interest you, which you want to explore further

- Driving more traffic to your platform or platforms, especially if you also sell products or services through them

- Creating a professional calling card that can help you switch careers, get that dream job or win a promotion

- Launching a business you are passionate about and have been thinking about for a while, but for which you have perhaps felt you did not have the relevant experience, until now, that is

- Wanting to teach and help others

- Creating an income stream

- [Insert your own] _____

_____

As you can see, a book can be a launchpad to a whole new world of opportunity if you leverage it correctly. So I invite you to stop here for a moment to think through and write down your reasons for wanting to produce a coffee table book, and what you aim to achieve by doing so. Once this is done, we will validate your reasons by taking some time to test the strength of your conviction by considering...

The Reasons Why You Should Not Turn Your Content into a Book

Not wishing to dampen your enthusiasm in any way, but this is also a good time to discuss some of the reasons why you should not turn your content into a book. Having just extolled the virtues of writing a book, I realize this could seem contradictory, but as the saying goes 'just because you can, does it mean you should?'

By opening up the publishing market to almost anyone, self-publishing has enabled talented writers and content creators, who might otherwise never have been found, to publish their own books. But on the flip side, self-publishing has also resulted in a glut of books, exhibiting varying degrees of quality, being published on every topic imaginable. This means that competition for eyeballs and the opening of wallets is fierce, so you owe it to yourself and your readers to produce the best possible coffee table book that you can, and stand out from the crowd.

This makes it extremely important to **do your homework before jumping in to create your manuscript**. And by homework, I mean research: researching your audience, the market, your competitors' titles, and so forth. Your book idea may seem wonderful to you, but your intended audience may think otherwise. And remember, you cannot always bank solely on your platform audiences for sales. They are used to getting content from you for free and could prove harder to sell to than someone who has never read or seen your content before. If your preliminary research shows that your proposed topic only interests a handful of people, then you need to consider if you want to spend all that time writing and producing something that has a high chance of not being bought, let alone read. I will expand on market research in Part Two: Doing Your Market Research.

Jumping on a trend bandwagon is not always a good idea, especially if you are going down the traditional publishing route, the reason being that you need to get your timings right. If you pick up the trend when it is well underway, a) it is likely you will not get a deal because publishers keep an eye on trends; and b) if you do get a deal, by the time your book is published it may no longer be relevant, which means the market will no longer be interested, no matter how good your book may be.

But one of the biggest reasons not to turn your content into a coffee table book is if your goal is solely to make money. As with anything you do, pursuing money as the be-all and end-all, over the value you can offer to others, will cloud your judgment and could lead to disappointment, resentment, and regret if things do not turn out as you hoped. Yes, one of your reasons may be to earn an income, but for many authors it is the purpose behind writing a book that proves to be the driving force. And you could, in fact, end up spending more money on producing and publishing your coffee table book than you make back on sales.

This is why it is important to give yourself a reality check.

The Realities of Publishing a Coffee Table Book

Almost every author and would-be author dreams of creating the next bestseller, which will fly off the shelves. Reaching the lofty heights of writers like J.K. Rowling and earning a vast fortune in royalties by selling a million-plus copies is a dream harbored by many authors; but this is the exception, not the norm. You would be wise to remember that, as unimaginable as it seems now, the first book in the bestselling series, *Harry Potter and The Philosopher's Stone*, was rejected by twelve publishing houses, and the first print run was only 500 hardback copies. Success came much later.

It is good to have dreams, self-belief and confidence, otherwise, how would innovation happen? So hold onto your dreams, but do give yourself a reality check every once in a while, especially as the publishing industry can be ferocious at times.

Selling 100,000 copies is said to be exceptional, and even managing to sell 20,000 is pretty good going, so the sad reality is that many authors struggle to make a living from writing books alone, and just manage to sell a few hundred copies at best. But there are exceptions. In 2021 designer and boutique hotelier Meryanne Loum-Martin shared on her Instagram page the news that her coffee table book *Inside Marrakesh* had sold 10,000 copies in 7 weeks and was headed for a reprint. In 2014, the YouTube star Zoella (Zoe Sugg) garnered attention for becoming the fastest-selling debut novelist since records began after her book *Girl Online* shifted 78,109 copies in just one week thanks to her massive online audience. I should point out that the attention soon shifted to the book allegedly having been ghostwritten. I will talk more about ghostwriting in Part Two: Planning Your Coffee Table Book – Ghostwriting.

This shows that, with the right combination of factors, it can be done. So, if you are determined to produce a book, coffee table or otherwise, do not let the stats put you off. I am not trying to pour cold water on anyone's dream. I just want you to be aware of the reality. You could be capable of penning the next bestseller, but you will never know if you do not try.

Moving beyond the stats, your book, like your platform, could be the start of bigger and better things, such as those you outlined in your reasons for wanting to publish a coffee table book. And whilst you may not end up making your fortune from the book itself, you can still leverage it to open up other income streams and get yourself in front of the decision-makers in your niche. This is what has happened to me.

The big rewards from writing a book for me have not been direct monetary gain, but rather the opening of doors to different opportunities. It has been said that having a book published is like having a very expensive business card – too true!

Since publishing my coffee table book, I have guest curated exhibitions, advised organizations interested in my niche, spoken at conferences and on panels, taught courses, mentored creatives, and become both a product sourcing editor and features writer for a lifestyle magazine, amongst other things.

For others, turning their content into a book has led to a whole range of opportunities, from speaking engagements to product partnerships, becoming consultants, coaches and more. Besides all this, the process of creating a coffee table book is an incredibly rewarding experience in itself, as nothing can beat the feeling of accomplishment that comes with seeing your hard work on a bookstore shelf or listed on Amazon!

So, as you can see, writing a book is not just about the money; it is an investment in your personal and professional development. But before you take the plunge there is still a bit more preparation to be done.

Producing a book demands a high level of commitment, periods of intense concentration, and difficult decision-making, especially when you are editing and having to decide what to keep and what to let go. Not to mention the fact that this process can be a solitary experience that requires you to put yourself in the right frame of mind.

Why You Need to Mentally Prepare Yourself for the Process of Publishing a Book

Writing and producing a coffee table book takes a lot of time and effort. Much like any other task which requires 100% and then some, the chances are you will end up becoming mentally exhausted from the effort. **This is why mentally preparing yourself for the task is very important.**

I also found the process to be highly emotional, and a draining experience at times. Whilst I was excited about my book, there were times when I would find myself being overcome with periods of self-doubt, thinking: 'What if no-one likes it?' 'What if it is not good enough?' 'What makes me think that I can write a book when I am not a writer in the traditional sense?' 'What if no-one buys it?' And on and on and on. These are very real fears. But when you choose to turn fear around, it can become a motivator. So do not dismiss your fears, rather acknowledge each one and neutralize them with positive comebacks.

It was important for me to know what I was letting myself in for before I started. I made sure I did some research to gauge what was currently happening in the publishing industry and to see if I could find out what to expect. The publishing process was unfamiliar to me and, added to this, not only was I writing a book, but as a former graphic designer, I was also designing it. I had to learn so many things as I went along, with very little support and relying heavily on search engines to point me to where I could find the information I needed. All I can say is, thank goodness for the Internet!

All this fact-finding helped me to put things into perspective and sort the dreams from reality. This book gives just one perspective of what to expect from producing a coffee table book, and the publishing process in general. I recommend reading a few others (but not too many or you will get overwhelmed by endless amounts of information) to help you reach an informed decision as to whether the process is for you. Speak to people in the industry if you have contacts. Find some websites, blogs and forums dedicated to book publishing. Spend a little time getting an idea of what to expect.

Make no mistake, writing a book is hard work. You will find yourself constantly thinking about it. My book stayed on my mind 24/7, and if you let it, it can consume you. However, despite the mental challenges, once I had got the hang of things, I enjoyed the process so much it did not feel like a chore. This, in turn, made it seem easier than it actually was, and gave me the confidence to self-publish my second book a year later. As with most big projects, good preparation and being well organized can make the publishing process smoother, especially if you are fitting it around a full-time job and/or family life. To organize yourself you will need to know how much time you can realistically commit to creating your book.

Finding the Time to Publish a Coffee Table Book

The time it takes to write, produce and publish a coffee table book depends on how much time you have to dedicate to the process. If you are a busy working parent running your platform on the side, you may not be able to set aside much time compared to a singleton who runs their platform as a full-time business. But no matter how much time you have to spare, **writing your book is more about maximizing your time than wishing you had more hours**. *Deepwork* by Professor Cal Newport is an insightful book about making the most of the time you have to accomplish your work that is worth reading.

Setting a Realistic Timeframe

Grace Bonney, of the popular (now closed) interiors blog Design★Sponge, is said to have written her second illustrative book *In the Company of Women* in two months. Another interiors specialist and bestselling author, Abigail Ahern, states on her blog that it took two weeks of intense writing to complete the first draft of her coffee table book *Colour*. Stephanie Mark and Jake Rosenberg, co-founders of Coveteur share that it took two years to take their book *The Coveteur: Private Spaces Personal Style* from idea to published.

With my first coffee table book, I had to coordinate, conduct interviews, write profiles and source the images for over fifty designer-makers, as well as interview several industry professionals scattered around the globe, all within an agreed timeframe of seven months to submit a completed manuscript. The timeframe was made possible because I had used my blog as a way of building my knowledge over several years.

So, as you can see, there are differences in the time it takes to produce and publish a coffee table book; but generally speaking, taking years to create a book is no longer the norm. The publishing process itself is another matter entirely, but more about that a bit later.

The publishing route you decide to take will dictate the time you need to write your book. If you are self-publishing, you can more or less publish whenever you are ready. If you are publishing the book traditionally, your contract will set out a mutually agreed manuscript submission date. So if you only have a few hours to dedicate to your book per week, bear this in mind when negotiating your contract.

I can't stress enough the need to **be realistic about your timeframe**. If it usually takes you a long time to plan, create and share your content, the same will be true of planning, writing and producing your coffee table book. Before I had a publishing deal, I thought it would take me three months to write a coffee table book, which was naive and overly optimistic. I began writing and researching the introduction to prepare myself before I even had a contract, and that alone took five months to get to a point where I had an acceptable first draft.

When setting deadlines for completing your book, you do not want to make them too long, as you will start to lose interest; and, likewise, you do not want to make them too short, as you will find yourself rushing to complete everything in time.

Producing a book does not always go to plan, think of the dreaded creative block. Do not force a book. I have had half-formed book drafts sitting in my Notes app waiting to be completed (and still have now). This book was one of them. I returned to it when I felt the time was right to do so. If you are struggling to complete your coffee table book, and going down the traditional publishing route, be upfront and tell your publisher sooner rather than later, as they will be more understanding about renegotiating deadlines earlier on.

There will be times, however, when you cannot afford to miss or renegotiate a deadline because of factors such as the book's publication date coinciding with an important event, riding the wave of a trend, or needing to get ahead of a rival publication. I will talk more about knowing the best time to publish your book in Part Two: Choosing the Best Time to Publish Your Book.

Having figured out how much time you have to commit to writing and creating your book you need to make those hours count.

Maximizing Productivity

To maximize the precious hours that you dedicate to creating your coffee table book, you need to find your rhythm and routine, and the best environment, whether that be the home office, library, park bench, coffee shop, a holiday let, or wherever else makes you feel comfortable and productive. Ask yourself, where do you usually produce your content, and would this space still work for you?

Discipline is important to help you stay the course, so create a schedule and stick to it.

Once you have written down your reasons for turning your content into a book, got yourself into the right frame of mind, and increased your determination to continue, it is time to start planning your coffee table book.

PART TWO:

Planning Your
Coffee Table Book

How successfully you can take your idea from content to a published book will depend on several factors. These include:

- **Topic:** what will your coffee table book be about?

- **Target audience:** who is going to buy and read your coffee table book?

- **Specifications:** what will your coffee table book look like?

- **Content considerations:** what are the words, images and illustrations making up your book's content?

- **Costs:** what are the costs involved in publishing a coffee table book, and how much will you need to spend?

- **Publishing options:** what type of publishing route will you end up taking?

It is good to work out these different areas before you start writing and creating your coffee table book, because knowing what to expect upfront can help you to minimize any problems that could occur further down the line. It will also help to keep the process flowing and avoid the overwhelming pressure that comes with meeting deadlines and being unprepared.

The reasons why you want to publish a coffee table book, which you outlined in Part One, will determine your options and chances of success. So keep them in mind as you go along.

What Will Your Coffee Table Book be About?

Your topic is your area of focus, and if you already have a firm idea of what you want your coffee table book to be about, you can head straight to Part Two: Doing Your Market Research, which looks at researching your book idea's suitability for your market. But if you have not decided on a topic just yet, not to worry, as this chapter will help you to identify a suitable topic, or topics, as the case may be. My blog brought forth ideas for several coffee table books and I suspect many platforms, be they blogs, podcasts, video or social media channels, will probably do the same.

Start by setting aside some time to go through your content and categories. Make a list of topics you would be interested in exploring in more depth. As you go along, look at what your most viewed posts are and ask yourself why they are popular. Go through any comments left on your content, and see if there are any questions being asked that lend themselves to a coffee table book format. What about any discussions between commenters: do they raise interesting points you could address? If the same question(s) keeps coming up, it is a sign that you, and the market in general, are not addressing the issue properly, and it warrants a more detailed response. Another option for finding a suitable topic is to go through any audience emails, messages and conversations where either the same questions keep coming up or people are wanting to know more about the topic.

Once you have a list of topics, write down a couple of sentences next to each one, stating why you think it would make a good book and how it would benefit your reader. Include some initial ideas of how you could develop the topic further.

Next, number each topic in order of preference. If you find yourself hovering between multiple categories, you could consider blending them, e.g. travel and food could become either a traveler's cookbook or a cookbook inspired by travel.

Choose the top ones that you want to explore further. I would recommend no more than three.

Why it is Not a Good Idea to Publish Straight from Screen

If you are seriously considering publishing a professional coffee table book, hitting print or download on all your posts and then binding up the pages will not suffice. Not all of your content will be suitable for a coffee table book. Unless, that is, you just want to create a hard copy format of your content for yourself, or to give to family and friends.

If you want your existing audience to buy your book, you need to offer them something more than what they already get from you for free. **You want your coffee table book to complement your platform, to provide additional value to the reader, and to inspire them or help solve their problems**. Never-before-seen content will encourage your audience to buy your book.

Although I had plenty of content to work with, which provided the starting point for my book, it needed to be expanded upon, revised, edited and fact-checked, meaning I needed to do further research and to verify the information. As I mentioned in Part One: Why Turn Your Content into a Coffee Table Book?, doing so can enable you to expand on a specific area, flesh out your posts and show off your expertise.

Even if your blog or social media platforms, such as Instagram, are more image than text-based, you still need to edit and organize to make the content presentable and relevant to the reader in a coffee table book format.

Your topic will also influence the type of coffee table book you will publish.

Types of Books

There are many different types of books, such as:

Fiction: novels, genre fiction (e.g. western, gothic, romance, historical, mystery and horror), novellas (a short novel or long short story), poetry, picture and pop-up books for children, graphic novels, comics.

Non-fiction: how-to guides, illustrative artbooks, coffee table and photography books, which are predominately image-led, directories, workbooks, coloring books, cookbooks, annuals, diaries, notebooks, monographs (specialized, often scholarly books profiling a single subject in microscopic detail), opinion pieces, essays on art or literature, biographies, memoirs, journalism, historical, scientific, technical, and economic, amongst others.

All of this means there are a number of directions your book could go in. Keep in mind that a coffee table book format is not solely reserved for non-fiction; a novella or comic, for example, could be presented in a coffee table book style.

Once you have a good idea of what you want your coffee table book to be about, the next step is to research the topic or topics if you have several to choose from.

Doing Your Market Research

So many would-be non-fiction authors skip market research, and instead launch straight into the process of writing and creating their book. Researching your idea before you start is important because it enables you to validate your idea for the market, and for target audience suitability. If you are planning to send a proposal to a traditional publisher they will want some of this information as proof of suitability and to show why they should publish your book. Doing research allows you to review and compare your idea against what is out there in terms of:

- **Trends:** will your idea be the first in setting a trend, or is the market already saturated?

- **Potential customers:** who else will your idea appeal to other than your existing audience?

- **Coffee table books already on the market that are similar to your idea:** spotting any gaps that your book could fill, especially for niche topics. (My book, for example, was on contemporary design from Africa and a trawl of bookstores and online retailers highlighted a glaring gap in the market)

- **Price ranges:** your book should be competitively priced so that it fits in with what is expected in its particular market category

Your research does not have to be a long and complicated process, requiring access to special reports and tools. Leading online book retailers, such as Waterstones (UK), Barnes & Noble (US) and, of course, Amazon, are effectively search engines and, as such, are highly useful tools for finding out the existing and soon to be published coffee table books in your category. Check the websites, blogs, podcasts, video channels, and social media accounts of the relevant publishers in your niche for their coming soon/new releases announcements, as well as their existing catalog of titles. When you have a few names, visit the authors' websites, as they will have more detailed information and may have content with even more information about their books.

Get out from behind the screen and pound the pavements. I did some of my research the old-fashioned way by visiting bookshops and libraries to see what was on the shelves and to visualize the category where my book would sit. This exercise is also helpful for tasks such as designing covers, choosing a book size, deciding on hardcover or paperback format, looking at price points, the average number of pages and various other factors related to producing your coffee table book.

It helps to see the company your coffee table book will keep online or in-store because your book needs to fit in with other coffee table books in its category. "But I thought that the whole point is to stand out from the crowd!" I hear you say. Well, yes it is, to a certain extent; however, there is the matter of consumer behavior, which is often influenced by people's perceptions of what a certain product type or category should be like.

Other avenues for research include asking around for opinions on your idea. Not friends and family, unless you can trust them enough to tell you the truth and not just what you want to hear. If you have access to your audience through a shop or an event, ask them in person. Use meet-ups, conferences, networking events, online groups and forums to gather information about your idea, either from direct conversations or snippets of conversation filling the air. You do not have to give away what you are planning to do, simply ask the questions you need the answers to. Perhaps add a survey to your platform or send it to your mailing list.

If you do not already do so, consider using sites like Pinterest for inspiration, as they are useful if your book is going to be more image-based. I found that Pinterest's hidden boards feature was a great way to build mood boards without broadcasting to the world what I was doing.

When you've explored them further, the chances are that not all of your selected topic ideas will have market potential, and that is fine. At least you will know before you start that you would have wasted time writing and producing any of them. Think back to Part One: The Reasons Why You Should Not Turn Your Content into a Coffee Table Book.

You may have an idea that is close to your heart, one you really feel passionate about, but perhaps your research has shown that there is not enough interest. This doesn't mean never creating and publishing it, but you might choose to put it aside for the moment in favor of another topic your research has revealed that would be timely, fresh and exciting, and allow you to become a thought-leader in your niche.

In a TV interview, British TV chef Jamie Oliver stated that he wrote his vegetable-based cookbook *Veg* eight years before it was published, but he could not convince the production company and his publisher to produce the TV show and publish the accompanying book because veganism was not mainstream at the time. He did not give up on his idea, but put it aside instead, and published other cookbooks in the meantime. Then, as the vegan lifestyle grew in popularity, the right time to publish it presented itself.

Help, There is a Similar Coffee Table Book Already Being Published!

What if you find out that there is a coffee table book similar to yours in production? Don't panic! When you panic you make emotional, not practical decisions.

You have several options. First, find out as much as you can about the book, its publication date and so on, and get a feel for the book's focus. Use this information to identify how your book can offer something different, or better, then be flexible about developing your idea.

If you are further along in the process, you could consider bringing your publishing date forward, holding back a bit on publishing until the attention on the other book dies down, or waiting to see if there are any significant industry-related events happening with which you could align your book launch to capitalize on the interest generated. For example, if you are publishing a coffee table book on vintage motorcycles of the early twentieth century and know there is a major exhibition coming up, you could use the buzz to introduce your book and pitch the relevant press stories.

Whatever you decide, remember that at the end of the day **what will make your coffee table book special is the unique perspective you can bring to your subject.** So use this to help your book stand out.

Choosing the Best Time to Publish Your Coffee Table Book

The speed with which books can be published has changed publishing. Traditional publishers who used to have control of publishing dates have now been forced to speed up in order to keep up with the rapid shifts in the market. If they don't, they risk being left behind. That said, for traditional publishers, knowing when to publish comes down to experience, such as knowing the market and having the benefit of a publishing calendar. This is planned out months or years in advance by the various departments who get together to decide a suitable publishing date for each book the publishing house signs. That is why many celebrity biographies are published in time for the Christmas shopping season, to target gift shoppers, romance novels are launched around Valentine's Day, and self-help, self-development, and fitness books come out in December/January in time for our New Year's resolutions.

One of the most important times in the annual publishing calendar is near the beginning of October, when a flurry of books by the main publishers and well-known authors are published in a bid to target the lucrative Christmas market. As such, a suitable publishing date may seem obvious in hindsight but it is easy not to give it much consideration beforehand when you are caught up in the excitement and are impatient to see the fruits of your labor.

With self-publishing, you could, in theory, publish any time you want. But knowing the right time goes back to two questions: a) why are you publishing your coffee table book in the first place? and b) what does your market research tell you? For example, do you want it to coincide with a special date, such as Mother's Day or Fashion Week; or is it because you are speaking at an important event in the coming year and would like to have a book out a few months beforehand? This would help to boost both your personal profile and sales, if the plan is to sell your book at the event. On the other hand, a similar coffee table book could be about to be published, or maybe a shift in news or policy could make it inappropriate to publish your book at that particular time.

A useful tip is to look at the publication date of published coffee table books in the same category as yours. This is usually found on online booksellers' platforms below the title and next to the author name. Do they have a particular month in common? If so, do a little more digging to find out why this is the case to help inform your decision.

As you can see, there are many reasons for choosing the best time to publish your coffee table book, but they are not all time-sensitive. This is the key advantage for self-publishers as it means you can more or less hit publish (digital or print) as soon as you are done, should you choose to.

Now that you know what type of coffee table book you are looking to publish, the topic you are going to write about, and when you are planning to publish it, the next thing to consider is the book itself.

How Will Your Coffee Table Book Be Structured

Plan out the structure and specifications of your coffee table book before you start writing and producing it, as this will help pave the way for a smoother and more productive process. Information about the structure is also good to know when you are negotiating your contract if you are planning on publishing with a traditional publisher. This is a question that will come up, particularly with regards to non-fiction and coffee table books. And if you are self-publishing, knowing your coffee table book structure and its specifications upfront will help to keep you on track and to budget.

Structuring Your Coffee Table Book

The structure of a coffee table book is simply the relevant sections that make up a book. These are divided into:

- Front Matter

- Main Body of the Book

- End Matter

Front Matter

The front pages of your book which comprise:

Half-title page: the first page of your book, which displays the title of your book only, no subtitles, bylines or author name(s).

Title page: the second page of your book, which displays the full title of your book, including subtitles, bylines, author name(s), co-authors, illustrator name(s), translator name(s), publisher's logo, and any other relevant logos you need to add.

Copyright page: this asserts your rights as the author of the book, lists the place and year the book was published, the edition number, ISBN, the publisher, permissions, and the printer (optional). It can also include a disclaimer and a list of other books you have published.

Dedication page (optional): the names of who you are dedicating your book to.

Contents page: (primarily for non-fiction books) this lists the different sections of your book with the relevant page numbers for easy reference. Chapters must be listed according to the exact wording used in the main body of the book and not just as numbers.

No page numbers are displayed on these pages.

Main Body of the Book

Foreword (optional): an introduction to your book, comprising complimentary words about you, the author, usually endorsing both your credentials and ability to be the one to write a book on the subject, and the relevance of such a book. A foreword is usually from someone prominent, so getting your granny to write some words would be sweet but a no-no unless she happens to be a well-known figure in the subject area.

Preface (optional): an introduction written by you, explaining in brief why you wrote the book. The preface can include a list of acknowledgments/thank yous.

Content: this is the book itself, comprising the chapters and their contents.

Page numbers are displayed on these pages.

End Matter

The back pages of your book comprising, as applicable to your book:

References page: a list of any sources of information you have researched, read and referenced or quoted for your book.

Further reading page: additional books or other sources of information recommended by you, the author, to readers interested in finding out more about the subject of your book.

Image credits page: copyright information for any images you have been granted the copyright holder's permission to reproduce in your book.

Drawings, tables, maps, and other illustrations page: copyright information for any other material you have been granted the copyright holder's permission to reproduce in your book.

Directory page: an alphabetical list of individuals or organizations featured or mentioned in your book, providing relevant contact information, such as a location or website URL.

Glossary page: an alphabetical list giving the meaning of certain words used throughout your book, rather like a dictionary.

Index page: an alphabetical list of keywords, phrases, and names used throughout your book, which reference the pages on which they can be found for quick access.

Acknowledgments page: the author's thank yous to those who assisted with producing the book. Depending on your layout this information can be included in the front matter pages.

Author bio page: information about the author of the book. This section can also be included in the front matter pages.

No page numbers are displayed on these pages.

Your Coffee Table Book Specifications

Once you have a structure that you are happy with, you will need an idea of your coffee table book's specifications. A book specification is what you want your finished book to look like. It is the information you would give to your developer, in the case of digital books, or your printer to a) get a quote for printing costs, and b) give them the information needed to prepare for the printing process.

A book specification comprises:

Format: this is whether your book will be published as a printed copy, digital version, or both.

Book size: this is the closed front cover dimensions of your book, taking into account height, width, and depth (spine). Coffee table books tend to be oversize to make the most of images and create an impression. Book size is not limited to a portrait rectangular shape. Coffee table books come in different shapes and sizes including square and even circular, as seen with Toots' coffee table books about different ball games, each shaped to resemble the respective ball.

Page count: this refers to the number of pages in your book and relates to printed books, in particular the cost effectiveness of litho printing (I talk about litho printing in Part Three: The Publishing Process: What to Expect – Output). The bound pages in a print book are based on multiples of four. Page 1 is the first printed page and always starts on the right-hand side. Depending on the overall page count, printers set up the pages on large sheets of paper in blocks of 8, 16, or 32. Once printed, the large sheets of paper are folded and gathered together in groups known as signatures, which are collated and bound to the cover, and then trimmed on three sides to open up the pages for flipping. The multiples of four rule differs slightly for hard cover case bound books. This is due to the application of endpapers which contribute to the page count, which means that the first printed page starts on page 3 on the right-hand side. The number of pages in your book is important because if your pages total up to an odd number, you will end up with an unintended blank page somewhere in your book. So when planning your book your final page count needs to be divisible by four. A good printer will let you know if your page count is an issue. Coffee table books can have as few as 32 to well over 256 pages.

The page count will also inform the width of your book's spine. This is essential to know when designing the cover, to ensure a perfect fit with no gaps when your book pages are bound to the cover. The more pages you have, the bigger the spine width, which can make a book more sturdy. However, the higher the number of pages, the more your book will cost to print. A publisher, in agreement with you, will set your word count and the number of pages and images. If you are self-publishing you will need to decide this yourself. Word count and number of pages helps to keep you focused, keeping you on brief and within budget. If you are printing-on-demand, the multiple of four page count rule doesn't usually apply, there may, however, be exceptions, so always check first before printing.

Number of images: this is the total number of images being featured in your book. Your book size, page count, and layout design will dictate the number of images that will work best in your book. The number of images in your book will also inform the metadata. (I go through metadata in Part Four: Promotion – Metadata.)

Type/color specification of images: the type of images you choose to display will dictate the print cost. Images can be full color, single color (monotone), two colour (duotone), black and white, or a combination.

Paper type: the stock and weight of the paper that the interior pages of your book will be printed on.

Cover binding: this refers to the type of cover your book's inner pages are bound to. A book will either have a hardcover or softcover (paperback) finish. A hard cover is known as case binding. Pages are sewn to the spine of the heavy board cover. Endpapers are used to hold the case bound cover in place. Case binding is the strongest and most expensive binding for books. Perfect binding is used for softcover books whereby a sheet of heavy paper is wrapped around the collated pages, which are then attached to the inside cover spine with a layer of adhesive. A perfect bound cover is not as durable as case binding, however, finishes such as lamination can add a layer of durability. Perfect binding is a cost effective option and is much quicker to produce than case bound.

Special cover treatments: this is the finish applied to the cover and includes dust jackets, gloss or matte laminate finishes, embossing and metallic foiling, to name a few. A slipcase is a separate protective box-like cover with one open end into which a book is inserted to help protect it.

Endpapers: these are the double-size sheets of paper at the beginning and end of a case-bound book, where one half is pasted to the inside cover and the other half forms a page. Endpapers are added to help to stablize and strengthen the book cover. The first right-hand page of an endpaper counts as the first page of a hardcover book. If you choose case-bound, do keep in mind that your actual page count starts at page 3. Endpapers can be blank white sheets, solid color or printed with logos, monograms or other relevant graphics.

Number of copies: the more copies you print, the cheaper the cost per book.

Other specifications that are not required by the printer, but will either be factored into your publishing contract, or come in handy for distributing and promoting your book are:

- Language

- Number of words

- Retail price

NOTE: Specifications are not set in stone. Whilst it is not ideal, changing your mind can and does happen as your book develops, although this could prove difficult if you are working with a publisher. If you are self-publishing then you can do what you like. I had a self-published coffee table book being proofed at the printers when I felt I needed to change the dimensions. It cost me to do so, but not as much as it would have had I let it be printed and been unhappy with the final result.

Planning your book also takes into consideration how you intend to produce the content within its pages.

Content Considerations

Content primarily refers to the imagery and text that forms your subject matter. Planning and creating your content may begin before, during or after you have decided the theme and vision for your finished book, so, if you are publishing traditionally, you don't have to wait for a publishing deal to start gathering and writing the content for your book.

Being visually led, imagery will be the most important content required for your coffee table book.

Finding and Selecting Images

Images are what make a coffee table book desirable. Coffee table books rely heavily on good professional photography or illustrations as their primary selling point. The images you use will set the tone for your book, determining the overall visual aesthetic.

Original photography or illustrations that you create yourself, or commission a photographer or illustrator to produce, offer exclusivity. Never-before-seen imagery can increase the value of your book. However, not all content creators are skilled photographers who take or create their own images.

Commissioning Imagery

When commissioning imagery you enter into a contract with the photographer or illustrator, and there are some things to be aware of with regards to copyright and licensing.

Hiring a photographer to take images for you does not mean you automatically receive the rights to use the images. A photographer retains the copyright for the images they have taken, and you still need to get permissions to use them. Many photographers work on the basis of a standard fee which pays for the photoshoot. You are then required to pay a fee for each image you select from the contact sheets. The fee depends on what you will be using the image for, so digital, press, print, foreign language edition and so forth. All these uses can attract a different fee level. This is sometimes referred to as licensing.

If your book gets published in several countries, you need to know if you would still have the rights to use the image, or if you have to pay separate fees for use in each edition. If the latter, rising costs could quickly cancel out any profit you were hoping to make. This is where the terms in contracts and licensing agreements are very important, even if you have been given permission to use an image free of charge.

When working with a photographer, always check and double check what usage rights the photographer's fee includes. For example, unless a photographer assigns full copyright for any usage over to you, their image fee may only cover digital usage and you will have to pay extra for print usage. So, when entering into an agreement, do negotiate for the full image rights, across all possible current and future uses, to be assigned to you.

This commissioning guidance also applies to working with an illustrator or other creatives to create your content, the slight difference being that illustrators tend to request an upfront flat fee along with royalties.

Commissioning imagery can incur significant costs. For example, if you are commissioning photography, bear in mind that in addition to the photographer, a stylist may be required to help set up the shots, which will impact your budget. So, as an alternative, you might source images from third parties, for example, an interior designer who has their own professional images and would be willing to grant you limited 'free-to-use' copyright in exchange for the exposure. The downside of this approach is no exclusivity. Free use of imagery can be negotiated by getting the copyright holder to sign an image release permission form, granting the use of the images for your book and any related promotional activity. This is what I had to do for my book *Contemporary Design Africa*, as I didn't have the budget to commission all the photography I needed.

Other image options include sourcing images from a photographer's existing work or from stock photography agencies, both of which can be less expensive if available as royalty-free. Royalty-free refers to paying once for an image without having to pay everytime you use it. Another option is using online stock photo libraries that offer copyright or royalty-free images for commercial use under Creative Commons (CC) licenses. A CC is issued when a creator gives people the right to share, use or edit works that they have created free of charge.

The next important content for consideration is your text, which is there to support your images and help put things into context.

Producing the Text

Text refers to the written words of your book. The amount of text you choose to have in your book depends on the style and type of book you are creating.

Some coffee table books have no, or minimal words, relying solely on images to convey the message. Other books may contain several pages of text for the preface or introduction sections, others may include paragraphs of text at the beginning of chapters, or may have text present throughout the book. It all depends on your subject and what you have to say about it.

Even if your book contains no paragraph text, you may still need to consider text in the form of captions, titles and headings.

If you are publishing your book traditionally, the publisher will set an agreed word count for your text. Word count is important as it contributes to the number of pages and layout your book will have. This information is also useful for self-publishers to help them plan their book's specification. Artbooks don't tend to have high word counts, typically less than 50,000, in comparison to novels, which can average 70,000–100,000 words.

However, not all content creators are writers who have a way with written words. You could be a vlogger or podcaster who prefers speaking into a microphone to typing on screen. This means that in order to create your book's written content you may need to use writing aids such as speech-to-text apps or transcription services. You could also consider engaging the services of a professional writer to plan and write your text for you. The practice of having someone write your book is known as ghostwriting, which has often been seen as bit of a murky area of book publishing.

Ghostwriting

Once frowned upon in publishing circles, ghostwriting has come out of the shadows and is now a common, widely-acknowledged industry practice. Ghostwriters are used by politicians, celebrities, and other notable figures to write speeches, books and other material. However, you don't have to be a well-known personality to use a ghostwriter.

Why would you consider using a ghostwriter?

- If you struggle with writing. Not everyone has writing skills, and you may require the help of a writer or journalist to get your words down on paper

- If you are time poor

- If you are writing in a language that is not your mother tongue

- If you have a learning disability such as dyslexia

While it is acceptable to use a ghostwriter, going down this route does raise questions over integrity and ethics. The main reason for this is that, in the past, ghostwriters were never usually credited for writing a piece of work, instead the attributed author would take all the credit by claiming the text as their own work. In present times, authors who do engage the services of a ghostwriter openly acknowledge the fact. So, in the interests of transparency, if you do work with someone to write your copy and have no input beyond explaining your ideas, don't then claim the written work as your own. Trying to pass off someone else's words as your own is unethical. Give credit where credit is due. Depending on the terms of agreement this can be in the acknowledgments section of your book, or even on the cover credits, where they would be presented as the writer or co-writer. So, something along the lines of 'words by Susie Grey', or 'written in collaboration with Susie Grey'.

How Ghostwriting Works

Best practise when working with a ghostwriter to write your copy is to make it a collaborative process. A ghostwriter will start by getting to know you and the subject of your book. When choosing a ghostwriter, look for someone who listens to you, gets what you want to say and can capture your tone-of-voice. Also ask for examples of the ghostwriter's work to get a feel for their style. Should you agree to work together, the partnership is then based on a series of interviews to capture your thoughts, ideas and words, which the ghostwriter then uses, along with carrying out additional research, to create the text. Interviews can be in person, online or over the phone. Expect a lot of back and forth as you review the text, and don't be afraid to make and suggest edits until you have a manuscript that you are happy with.

Ghostwriters do not work on a royalties basis, nor are they entitled to royalties. They typically charge a flat fee to write your book. Depending on several factors, including the level of input and the number of words, you can expect to pay around £/US$6,500–£/US$25,000 for a ghostwriter. That said, some ghostwriters may request royalties on top of their flat fee, which will in turn affect the amount of royalties you will receive per copy.

How to Find a Ghostwriter

If you are publishing traditionally, your publisher will assign a ghostwriter to your book. Depending on your contract, you may be charged for retaining the services of the ghostwriter. This could be calculated against your royalties, billed as a separate charge, or affect the amount of advance you are offered.

If you are self-publishing, methods for finding a ghostwriter include publishing industry and editor directories, word-of-mouth recommendations, and search engine and social media searches. Solicit recommendations from your network, online communities, relevant industry directories, and events such as publishing conferences, book fairs, and festivals. You could also look for names mentioned in the acknowledgments section of books similar to yours. The responsibility for negotiating the fee will be down to you, based on the agreement you reach with the ghostwriter.

Costs of Publishing a Book

There is a myth that self-publishing a digital book costs nothing. That is not true. No matter what your book's format or publishing route is, from having your manuscript edited to bookseller platform fees, there is definitely some level of cost involved. So then, how much does it cost to publish a coffee table book? Well, to use a cliché, how long is a piece of string? In other words, there is no specific production cost for each book. It is true that **publishing a coffee table book, or any book for that matter, can end up costing you more than you make back in royalties or sales**.

In today's publishing environment, authors are having to adopt a business mindset, regardless of whether they publish traditionally, or via self-publishing. Therefore, as a self-publisher, you become a business, taking on many of the costs typically borne by a publisher. This makes it important to figure out beforehand where you will need to spend money, to get an idea of prices, and to set an appropriate budget.

A budget will help the process to flow, and keep your book publication to schedule. Knowing how much you are willing to spend on producing your coffee table book will also help you decide which publishing route to take.

The cost of publishing a book means that crowdfunding has proven popular with self-publishers and independent publishers alike, as the campaign's backers help fund the production and print costs. Having customers already lined up to receive a copy also helps to negate costs such as storage.

To calculate the costs you will need to look at the following areas and set yourself a best-case and worst-case scenario:

- **Production:** editing and proofreading, design for print, and/or e-book development

- **Printing and distribution:** printing, shipping, and storage

- **Fees/Commissions:** the percentages taken by retailers, wholesalers, and distributors

- **Marketing:** the budget allocated to promoting your book

- **Indirect overheads:** phone bills, transportation

How Much Does it Cost to Publish a Coffee Table Book*

	Low	High
Editing	£300	£1,500
Proofreading	£250	£700
Layout design	£500	£3,600
Cover design	£375	£800
ISBN	£0	£89
Total	£1,425	£6,689
Printing**	£2,775	£5,675
Marketing	Free	£2,500
Final total:	£4,200	£14,864

*This calculation is based on 200 printed pages and a 20,000 word count, and excludes photography, image licensing and any other services specific to your book.

** Based on a 750–1,500 copy print run @ £3.70 per copy.

Even if you are traditionally publishing your coffee table book, you may incur personal costs that are not covered by an advance, such as travel for research purposes, having to take days off work outside your normal holiday allowance, or commissioning professional photography if you are the one providing the required images.

Another reason to know how much it will cost to publish your coffee table book is to enable you to set the correct retail price.

Pricing Your Book

It may seem strange to discuss how much your coffee table book will cost before you have even finished it. However, because your marketing and promotional efforts will start before your book is published, information such as the price needs to be established before then. This will enable you to buy the ISBN, generate your metadata, and create your cover, amongst other things, which I will cover in later chapters.

When you sign with a book publisher, they will already have a good idea of how much your book will cost. Again, this is based on experience and knowing the market. That said, pricing a book is not an exact science and is based on several factors. If you are self-publishing you will need to work this out based on your circumstances.

There are a couple of ways to price a book.

1. Top-Down Strategy

Your research will highlight the average price range for similar coffee table books with similar specifications in your category. These prices can be an indication of what your target readers will expect to pay. Books are not immune to consumer psychology, product perceptions and comparisons of what is deemed to be better. So you do not want to price your book out of the market by making it too expensive, nor do you want to price it so low that it negatively affects your credibility. This strategy is known as top-down.

2. Bottom-Up Strategy

The bottom-up strategy involves dividing your total costs by the quantity of books you plan to print and sell and then multiplying the figure by your markup to get your cost per copy. You will need to know, or have an estimation of, all the different costs upfront.

The formula would look something like this:

(Production + Printing + Distribution + Marketing) ÷ Quantity x Markup = Cost Per Copy

The markup takes into account the wholesaler, distributor, retailer and platform fees, and fluctuations in future printing prices, to ensure that you are left with some profit margin. Your markup is what you consider to be fair, based on the current costs and your projections, and can be anywhere from 2-10 times the amount. So if your book is to be distributed as digital only, your markup will not be as high as a printed book which has a more involved physical distribution chain.

Some bottom-up strategies will remove Production, i.e. editing, proofreading, and design, from the calculation as they are seen as one-off costs that spread themselves across the book's lifetime sales to the extent they are no longer relevant to the calculation.

Using and comparing both strategies to determine a realistic price that meets the market's expectations is a good idea.

The advantage of digital books is that you can tweak the price until you find the sweet spot, without having to take the book off the retail platform. Some digital book and print-on-demand publishing platforms, such as IngramSpark and Lulu, have a handy royalty calculator that will help you work out how much you receive per copy sold, based on a list of specifications, such as page size, number of pages, paper type, color, and potential price.

Self-publishers NOTE: if you are printing-on-demand, bear in mind that the printing cost can fluctuate in response to market changes, i.e. paper price increases due to shortages, which in turn will affect how much you will earn per book. Do keep an eye on this as you may need to update your book price accordingly.

Having a target price range for your book will help curb your production and printing costs, as the more you spend to produce your coffee table book, the less profit you will make. The costs involved will also help you to decide which publishing route works for you.

Publishing Options Available for Your Coffee Table Book

The publishing option you decide on will be dictated by several factors, including the type of book you are publishing, how quickly you want to publish, and how much production work you want to do yourself.

Making key decisions such as whether to publish one book or several, through traditional or self-publishing, and printed or digital, will enable you to move forward. But first, a bit of background on the publishing industry, to help put things into context.

The Publishing Landscape: A Brief Overview

The Global Book Publishing Industry

Book publishing is a highly competitive industry, one that is made up of traditional big-name publishers, smaller independent publishers, and self-publishers. The traditional industry has undergone significant change over the last two decades or so, impacted by the rise in digital books and self-publishing. This had initially seen a decline in the sales of printed books, but demand for printed books is said to be on the rise once more. Despite the initial growth in popularity of e-books, according to a Pew Research Center survey, printed books remain the most popular format for reading, as it appears readers still prefer reading print on the page, rather than on screen. However, the sales of printed books, are being impacted by the rise in popularity of audiobooks.

Coffee table books rely on specialist topics, and typically feature more images than text. Their value lies not just in the information contained within their covers, but in the quality of production, such as beautiful papers, tactile finishes, and high spec photography, to create objects of desire that attract readers and book collectors. Due to their collectable and decorative nature, coffee table books have so far withstood the impact of digital publishing and, as such, provide a more emotional connection that digital books cannot yet replicate.

Traditional Book Publishers

The global book industry is dominated by a handful of big-name publishers, referred to as the Big Five. The leaders are: Penguin Books and Random House, who merged in 2013 to form Penguin Random

House, Hachette, HarperCollins, Simon & Schuster, and Pan Macmillan. Leading educational publishers include Pearson, Oxford University Press, and John Wiley and Sons.

Traditional publishers were able to control the industry through their ability to order in bulk, which meant they could negotiate terms that were usually out of the reach of independent and self-publishers. This has changed dramatically as the global publishing industry has undergone a great transformation in the digital age, with print sales initially declining in the face of digital books and increased competition from online retailers, self-publishing authors and service providers, such as print-on-demand.

Online retailers like Amazon have not only enabled the production of cheaper books by undercutting booksellers, they have also impacted the publishing sector by creating their own self-publishing platforms, dealing a double whammy to traditional publishing.

Traditional publishers also have a reputation for looking after their big-name authors at the expense of new, unknown ones. This affects many aspects of the process, ranging from how much is invested in marketing, to the size of the advances and royalties offered. In addition, the terms of the publishing contracts issued have long been seen as unfavorable compared to the freedoms offered by self-publishing.

Traditional Coffee Table/Artbook Publishers

In addition to the traditional publishers, there are a number of publishers who specialise solely in the production and publication of artbooks. Global leaders in artbook publishing include Thames & Hudson, Phaidon, Taschen, Prestel, Rizzoli, Chronicle Books, Art/Books, Abrams, Artisan Books and the luxury book publishers Assouline.

Independent Publishers

Independent publishers, also known as the independent press, bridge the gap between traditional and self-publishing. They are similar to the traditional publishers model, but operate on a smaller scale and are far more flexible to market changes.

Advances in digital technology, such as print-on-demand and distribution agreements, mean that small independent publishers do not have to order in bulk or find storage for their books, the cost of which made running an independent press difficult in the past. Independent publishers can foster closer relationships with all their authors, unlike larger traditional ones, which tend to focus their attention on their big-name and celebrity authors.

Although independent publishers have to work harder to get their names known, they offer an alternative to self-publishing, providing a degree of professionalism by offering an imprint, or publishing name, under which an author's book can be published. For example, Rocket 88 is an imprint of Essential Works and Hoxton Mini Press is an independent publishing house and therefore an imprint. This is one of the main reasons some self-publishing authors set up their own independent publishing companies to publish their own titles.

Having proven themselves to be successful, independent publishers can catch the eye of established traditional publishers who, looking to diversify their offerings, capitalize on new audiences, and neutralize the competition, may make an offer to buy them. Independent publishers that have since been bought by traditional publishers include Black Dog Publishing and Jacqui Small, now an imprint of Quarto.

Setting up as an independent publisher

Setting up as an independent publisher is much the same as setting up a business. Choose your publishing name, select a suitable trading entity type, e.g. sole trader, company, partnership, and register with your local tax office. Once you've set it up, use the name to purchase and register your ISBNs. The ISBN identifies you as the publisher of your book, which I explain in more detail in Part Three: What is an ISBN and Do You Need One?

Self-Publishing

Digital technology has helped democratize the publishing industry, enabling anyone with an idea to publish their own book without having to go through a publishing house. E-readers, like the Kindle and Nook, smartphones and tablets have all enabled people to download and access books with ease. Digital books eliminate costly production processes and stock that gathers dust in warehouses, resulting in much cheaper books. If books need to be printed, print-on-demand services are available. With self-publishing, the amount you earn per copy tends to be higher, but self-publishing platforms are known to take a sizeable percentage for commission. Leading self-publishing companies are Amazon's Kindle Direct Publishing, Apple Books for Authors, IngramSpark, Blurb, and Lulu.

Vanity Publishing

Vanity publishing is a term referring to a publishing house that requires authors to pay a fee to have their book published. **A reputable publisher takes on the financial risk and will never charge you to publish your book.** In the days before self-publishing, vanity publishing was the only real option for authors rejected by publishing houses to publish their book independently. This resulted in an industry rife with scams and unfulfilled promises.

As self-publishing gives authors much better opportunities for publishing independently, vanity publishing companies have adapted to take advantage of technology, and have rebranded themselves as one-stop-shop self-publishing services to disguise the fact they are charging authors to publish their books. If you are thinking of taking the vanity publishing route, beware of the pitfalls and research the publisher thoroughly.

Traditional Publishing Versus Self-Publishing

When it comes to publishing your coffee table book you have a choice between traditional publishing and self-publishing routes, or a hybrid of both. Not everyone will get a publishing deal or choose to take it if they are offered one, as some prefer to self-publish instead. I have had the opportunity to experience both the traditional publishing and self-publishing routes, and each has its advantages and disadvantages. At the end of the day, it comes down to your expectations and what you want to achieve with your book.

Comparisons of traditional publishing and self-publishing

	WORKING WITH A PUBLISHER	SELF-PUBLISHING
ADVANTAGES	The credibility that comes with being associated with a recognized publishing house Receiving an advance Editorial and production support Marketing and promotion support Distribution services, storage, and getting a book into bookstores Access to expert advice, contacts and networks	You publish when you are ready Retain greater control over your work and vision Get to keep a greater percentage of royalties Retain all rights
DISADVANTAGES	Low royalties Restrictive contracts Limited creative control – disagreement over content, direction Long production process Marketing and promotion limited to a few months Your book is one of many that is being published at the same time	Lack of editorial and production support and expertise The steep learning curve of having to do everything yourself High costs, especially if printing Responsibility for legal issues, such as negotiating image rights, licensing, and quoting copyrighted information Difficulty getting accepted by distributors and stocked in bookstore It may be difficult to get noticed Exclusion from entering certain literary and industry prizes

Now for a look at each publishing option in more detail.

About Traditional Publishing

When seeking out a publishing contract, the traditional publishing process typically follows the path of finding a literary agent, creating a proposal or manuscript and then submitting it to a publisher. You can skip working with a literary agent and submit directly to your publisher of choice, but do bear in mind that some publishers do not accept unsolicited proposals or manuscripts.

What is the Role of a Literary Agent?

A literary agent is an intermediary between an author and a publisher. They support the authors they work with, in a variety of ways, including:

- Helping you to understand, and guiding you through the publishing process

- Protecting your interests by advocating on your behalf when negotiating contracts, drafts contracts, and advances with a publisher

- Working editorially to help you to develop your ideas into a presentable manuscript or proposal. This is great for those who may not be confident or skilled in expressing their thoughts in a written form. Depending on the type of book, this editorial support involves at least four rounds of editing drafts, and the process can take about a year

A literary agent and their agency will represent your work exclusively once you have signed with them, and a good literary agent will remain involved with you after publication.

One thing to note: literary agents have close ties with editors in publishing houses as they spend time in the same circles. As such, literary agents get to know what individual editors are looking for. Some editors prefer to work with certain literary agents and will recommend them to authors they are interested in signing.

When Should You Start Looking for a Literary Agent

The process differs slightly for fiction and non-fiction books.

For fiction books, it is recommended that you start looking for a literary agent once you have finished the first draft of your book. When contacting a literary agent you would typically be required to send three chapters and a synopsis. A synopsis is a summary of what your book is about, and is a chance to show your passion for your idea and sell it.

You need to finish the first draft because it increases the chances of a literary agent requesting additional chapters or even your entire manuscript. With fiction authors, having an existing platform or following is not a prerequisite for consideration.

Non-fiction is a different process, as you are required to send in a proposal for your idea and include a sample chapter. You will also be required to establish your credentials, in other words, why are you the best person to write a book on your proposed topic. Your credentials include awards, accolades, experience, your website, blog, social, any other platforms, books, and articles that connect you to your proposed topic.

Publishers want to see that you have built an engaged platform around your niche. This is not about the number of followers, although that can be a bonus, it is more about giving the literary agent and publisher confidence that you are knowledgeable in the topic you are wanting to create a book about and can provide proof of this.

Finding a Literary Agent

Literary agents work by building a list of authors who fit in with their priorities or area(s) of interest. Do your research to find out what you can about the literary agent you hope to work with before contacting them, and do not contact an agent who does not specialize in your subject area, as there is a high chance that you will not get a response.

Ways of finding a suitable literary agent include:

- Searching literary agency websites, as these tend to list profiles of their agents, highlighting which subject areas the person works in

- Recommendations from your network

- Identifying names mentioned in the acknowledgments section of books that would be in the same category as yours

- Attending relevant industry events such as publishing conferences, book fairs, festivals and book signings

- Researching social media, particularly Twitter

You should not have to pay for a literary agent to represent you. Literary agents work on commission, getting paid when their author gets paid. So beware of any person or agency requesting an upfront fee.

As previously mentioned, once you have found and signed up with a literary agent, they will facilitate the process of pitching your idea to publishers. If, however, you choose not to go through a literary agent, but want a traditional publishing deal, you will need to find and contact publishers yourself.

What is the Role of a Publisher?

A publisher buys the rights to an author's book with the aim of turning it into a financial success. When signing on with a publisher you will be under the care of an editor. Depending on the publishing house's size, this could be the person who bought your book, the person who recommended it for purchase or a senior editor specializing in your subject matter. The editor will take on the responsibility of project managing your book from concept to getting the finished product into the hands of readers.

Finding a Publisher

Finding a publisher is much the same process as finding a literary agent. You need to identify the publishers who specialize in publishing books in your subject area. The easiest way to do this is to get a publisher's name from the cover of a published book that is in the same category as, or in a similar style to, your proposed book, then look up their details and website.

Other ways of finding a publisher include:

- Attending relevant industry events, such as publishing conferences, book fairs, and festivals

- Your network, talking to other authors and content creators to get their recommendations

- Conducting a search engine search

Publishers themselves are always on the lookout for new talent and content, so they will do their own research, scouting for what is out there. Hence those content creators and self-published authors who get approached with a deal.

How Publishers Decide Which Books to Publish

Publishing is highly process-driven and made up of many individual departments that focus on specific areas of the acquisition, production and distribution chain. When it comes to deciding on and acquiring a book to publish, the process is loosely based on the following description, which is most typical of a big publishing house.

There are a few people within a publishing house who decide whether a book gets published. The process starts with editorial meetings where editors from the different publishing divisions come together to discuss the various books they are each interested in publishing. The bigger the publishing house, the more likely it is to contain divisions, each division having its own imprints with a dedicated editor or team of editors. Imprints are like sub-brands and are used to edit and market specific books to their relevant audience demographics. These meetings will also involve representatives of the key departments that have a say in the books acquired by the publishing house, namely: acquisitions, publicity, marketing, and sales.

In these meetings, the sales department will put forward their projections for how many copies they think each book will sell across the different categories of hardback, paperback, export, and so forth. This is important because **it is on the projected sales figures that an author's advance is calculated**.

Small or independent publishers may have a less elaborate set up combining several functions into one role.

Once you have a list of suitable publishers, you will need to review their submissions guidelines, then prepare and submit a proposal outlining the idea for your book, giving them the reasons why they should publish it.

Creating and Submitting Your Coffee Table Book Proposal to a Publisher

Most publishers will have some form of submissions policy on their website. If they are accepting submissions you will be directed to the relevant information. This is often hidden, so you may need to hunt around a bit before you find what you need.

If the publisher does not accept submissions, this is usually clearly stated, meaning you will have to go through a literary agent. However, if there is no submissions policy or page, check the FAQs. If there is nothing there then send an email to the general enquires or contact email address asking if they accept proposal submissions and, if so, how you can go about submitting a book proposal.

NOTE: Only send your completed manuscript when they ask for it! **Do not email or post unsolicited manuscripts**, especially if it is your only copy, as the chances are high that it will not reach the correct recipient and will most certainly end up being binned. This is:

a. For legal reasons. Reputable publishers will seek to protect themselves from being accused of copying an idea, so they will only request a completed manuscript once an offer has been made and contracts signed.

b. Because editors can receive around a minimum of six manuscripts or proposals a day, which may not seem like much at first consideration, but once you multiply the figure by five (number of days in the week), then by four (number of weeks in the month), this works out to 120 manuscripts a month! So you can see why it is important to get your proposal or chapter submission right.

Publishers accepting proposal submissions will most likely offer some guidelines to help you prepare your proposal. Read and follow them!

Creating a Proposal – What to Include

A proposal gives the publisher an idea of the book you want to publish. It is also an opportunity for you to further examine your idea before committing to developing the book. A proposal can help to flag up any issues. Even if you choose to self-publish, consider creating a proposal for yourself as a guide. I do this before writing my books. It helps to clarify my goals and guides the process.

Each publisher will have their specific requirements; however, there are commonalities, and a proposal will be a variation of the following structure:

Title page: what your book is about. Use your title to attract the publisher's interest, even if your title is provisional. For example, if your platform is about interior design, do not say: 'Proposal for a book about interior design.' Add more descriptive detail, e.g. 'Proposal for a book about interior design for small, awkward spaces'.

Introduction/Synopsis: a key point summary of your book idea, explaining why it is relevant, why it should exist, and so forth. You are writing to persuade a publisher to sign you. In terms of length, a page is best but try to make it no more than three pages.

Chapter outline: this shows the structure of your book. Include a brief paragraph explaining the content of each.

Sample chapter: take one of the chapters from your chapter outline and write a few paragraphs. This is important as it gives the literary agent and the publisher a feel for your writing style and tone-of-voice, which is important in deciding who is the target of your book, amongst other factors. **TIP:** Look to see if you have relevant content, e.g. blog posts, audio or image captions that you can rework into the paragraphs you need.

Sample images: if the selling point of your book is the imagery, include a selection of images to give the publisher an idea of the style and quality. If you use images that don't belong to you, make sure you credit the source and make it clear that they are not yours but are being used for illustrative purposes only.

About you: explain why you are the best person to write the book. Provide links to your channels, website, blog, podcast and social media platforms, as well as any PR you've received. Include your audience stats if you have a sizeable, engaged following.

CV/Biography: a relevant summary of your work, career, skills, qualifications, experiences, and achievements.

And before you rush off to submit your proposal remember that...

First Impressions Count

When submitting your proposal, a spelling and grammar check is of the utmost importance. A good publisher will assign editors to edit your work once you are signed with them, but first impressions count, so make the effort. Hire someone to edit your work if you have to. If money is an issue, get a skilled friend or family member to go over it, or use an editing app such as ProWritingAid, Grammarly or Hemingway Editor.

Also, take the time to format and present your proposal. Getting your work professionally laid out will create a good impression, particularly given the highly visual nature of coffee table books. This is important because, in the absence of a finished manuscript, the publisher needs to be confident that you can produce the book. Once again, call in favors from friends and family who are good at design or who may know someone who is. Or find a professional on services such as PeoplePerHour, Behance and UpWork. If you format it yourself and you are not a designer, design software and customizable templates from platforms such as Canva, Adobe Express and Creative Market, offer a solution. But if you feel yourself reaching for Comic Sans, drop the mouse and find a professional!

Remember not to go overboard. Keep it clean and simple.

Once you've submitted your proposal, the waiting game begins. Be patient, it can take several months before a publisher will get back to you. A rule of thumb is three months or so. Some publishers will have an auto-reply, or information on their website about estimated response times, to help manage expectations. If you have not heard back after a few months, you can consider your submission to have been unsuccessful at that particular time. Not all publishers will write back to let you know.

Handling Rejection

You have created a winning proposal and submitted it to your chosen publisher only to receive a response saying your proposal is not right for them because [insert reason] _____. Rejection happens. If you can ask for more detailed feedback then do so, as it will help you to improve your proposal the next time around.

Publishers reject proposals for a range of different reasons, including badly prepared documents and the subject not being their area of specialism. It may also be the case that your proposal was fine, but they are already publishing a similar book. Do not be disheartened, pick yourself up and try again. The proposal for my first book got rejected several times. I won't lie, rejection hurts! I gave in to the feeling by moping around for a few days, then sprang back up and refused to accept the rejection.

Interestingly, I tried the first, a small publisher because I feared rejection from the bigger, more prestigious ones. Then, after my first rejection, I contacted the bigger publishers and ended up publishing with one of them, which just goes to show how important it is to believe in yourself and your idea.

Keep in mind that getting a traditional publishing deal as a first-time author is notoriously tricky, so self-publishing is a route that some authors take to help them attract a traditional publisher and get a publishing deal, even if it is just for the foreign rights. Foreign rights are a license granted by the publisher who has bought and published your manuscript to overseas publishers, so that they can publish a local edition of your book in their country or region.

Publishers track self-published sales to find out who is doing really well. For a traditional publisher, a good self-published book that shifts copies equates to one worth investing in. It is not uncommon for a self-published book to attract a traditional publishing deal based on its initial success.

You've Received a Positive Response

You have a foot in the door, but you are by no means there yet. I received a positive response from my publisher within a month or so of having submitted my proposal. This was in April, but I did not sign my contract until December of the same year. I was initially asked to submit further supporting material in the form of images and was called in for a meeting. After that there was silence for about six or seven months. After plucking up the courage to contact them to find out if they were still interested in my idea, I went in for another meeting to discuss aspects of the book in more detail, including specifications and how long I would need to write and produce it, all of which were put into a draft contract that followed a few weeks later.

The Contract

A publisher interested in publishing your book will offer you a contract. Publishers' contracts are one of the main reasons many authors choose the self-publishing route. With terms favoring the publisher, contracts can be downright contentious. Before self-publishing, authors didn't have much of a choice when it came to negotiation until they entered the multiple bestseller group.

If you are offered a contract, it is wise to get a legal representative to look over it. You can get it vetted by organizations such as The Society of Authors, or ALLI in the UK, or The Authors Guild in the US.

Many publishers' contracts are based on boilerplate templates, meaning there will be sections that are non-negotiable, particularly when it comes to publishers protecting themselves against being sued for libel and plagiarism. Other things to look out for include clauses that seek to protect their investment in terms of costs and developing an author by including the first right of refusal for the author's next work; and, of course, royalties. In a nutshell, a traditional publishing deal offers little in the way of lucrative royalties unless you sell high volume, because the more copies you sell, the more you will make.

Royalties

Royalties are what you will earn per sold copy of your book. This is typically calculated on net receipts – what is left after distributors, wholesalers and others in the book-buying chain have received their commission. Royalties are the biggest bone of contention between authors and publishers. Royalties offered by big publishers typically fall into the range of 7.5% – 15% per copy, according to the author's status.

Contention stems from the myth that publishers give low royalties because they are greedy and you will make more money by self-publishing. This is misleading. Publishers spend a lot of money on publishing a book, and what they make back is not that high once the costs, including production, printing, promotion and retailer discounts, have been factored in. **Publishers rely on publishing multiple authors, selling rights and licensing, amongst other factors, to create profit**.

The chances are you will make more per copy sold by self-publishing, but you may not sell as many copies as a publisher would. This is due to their reputation, contacts, and reach, and it is something to consider.

Small and independent publishers, on the other hand, often pay much higher royalties. This is normally a goodwill gesture for not offering you an advance or, if they do, a very small one. Some may even go as high as 50% in exchange for the author bearing some of the production cost responsibilities on a partnership basis.

Advances

An advance is a sum of money offered to an author for the rights to publish their book. Offering an advance is a publisher taking a risk on the sales potential of a book. An advance is not an author's right, and some publishers, such as small independents, do not offer advances.

Advances have decreased significantly over the years and are typically not that much, ranging from £/US$1,000–£/US$25,000, especially if you are a first time and unknown author. High, six-figure or record-breaking advances make the headlines, which creates unrealistic expectations in the minds of would-be authors.

Interest from other publishers can create a bidding war that tends to drive up advance prices. A literary agent can invite editors from different publishing houses to bid on your manuscript if they think it will attract a high offer.

However, do not get hung up on attracting a big advance. While it is nice to receive some money upfront, an advance is like a loan, and you will receive no royalties until your book has generated the equivalent amount back in sales. This is referred to as earning out the advance.

Advances are usually paid out in installments. Typically, a third on signing, another third upon delivery of the completed manuscript, and the remaining third on publication. A small advance, therefore, has the advantage of giving you a chance to earn it out quicker and move on to earning royalties.

If you do not earn out your advance, i.e. your book does not sell enough copies, this could leave you in the position of having an unspoken 'debt' to the publisher, making it difficult to pitch a second book to them. Not to mention the difficulty of attempting to attract another publisher who may be reluctant to sign you because of this 'debt'.

I should stress that remaining balances on advances do not need to be paid back if you have not sold enough copies. However, for peace of mind and legal protection, get this in writing in your contract. **NOTE:** Not having to pay back an advance will not apply if you breach any of the relevant terms outlined in your contract on which your advance is dependent.

Rights

If a publisher in another country is interested in publishing your book in their locality and potentially in their own language, the original publisher will sell them the rights to do so. The rights contract would grant them a license to print the book, with a percentage of the sales going to the original publisher. The author then receives royalties based on that percentage, which would be lower than the standard royalty. If you self-publish, you can use a platform like PubMatch or sign with a publisher on a rights-only agreement.

Another important area to consider when signing contracts is copyright.

Copyright

Copyright is the process of having, or giving someone, legal permission to use, reproduce, print, publish and distribute your work. Copyright of your text and images, if these are taken by you, remains with you. By signing the contract you are granting the publisher permission to print and use your text in the book they are creating, and for any related promotion. Any images you have supplied that are either used in the book or for promotion will indicate the copyright details you provide. If any images are supplied by a third party, you need to obtain their signed permission for use if they own the copyright. If they don't own the copyright, you will need to find out who does and get their permission for use. The publisher will have copyright over the design and layout of the book.

The contract is a legally binding agreement. As such, I strongly recommend seeking legal advice before putting pen to paper, or getting a literary agent who can advise you and negotiate a good deal on your behalf.

About Self-Publishing

If, however, you want greater control over publishing your book and potentially a bigger chunk of the per sold copy profit, then self-publishing could be the option for you.

Self-publishing works well for specific niches that fall outside of the traditional publishing focus, as well as for authors who know exactly where their audience is and what they want. It is therefore important to get clued up on metadata, analytics, and SEO, which gives professional content creators a built-in advantage. These are things that I discuss in Part Four: Promotion.

The stigma of self-published books not being proper books still lingers. In response, some self-publishing authors choose to set up a registered self-publishing company to give an air of professionalism and set themselves apart from the crowd.

PART THREE:

The Publishing Process, What to Expect

In this section, we will look at the traditional and self-publishing book production processes in closer detail. This includes:

- The different stages of both publishing options

- A walk through the self-publishing production process

- How your book will be published in terms of physical and digital output

- Distribution and how you will get your book into the hands of your readers

What to Expect When Working with a Publisher

You've signed a publishing deal. Congratulations! Take some time to celebrate. Your preparation and perseverance have paid off and now you can get down to either starting or submitting your completed manuscript. Upon submitting your manuscript, the publisher may require proof of manuscript copyright from the author in the form of a signed document stating the fact. This is to confirm that you are in indeed the owner of the work being submitted, and have the necessary permissions to reproduce any third-party content you have included. Proof of manuscript copyright enables the publishing process to move forward.

How you proceed will be determined by what you agreed in your contract. A traditional publisher carries the burden of production and print and, apart from editing, you will rarely be heavily involved in this part of the process. You will be assigned a project manager who will be the point of contact between you and the different departments involved at each stage, which are as follows:

Editing

Your manuscript will go to the various editors for several rounds of copy-editing, editing, fact-checking, proofreading. You will be required to review and approve each round, typically three or four rounds.

Design and Layout

The in-house design team will design your book and you will have input. High-profile books, or those requiring complex design solutions, are often outsourced to specialist book design professionals or design agencies. As someone who has a graphic design background, it was agreed that I would design and lay out my book. I found this beneficial as I could be at the center of my book's development, giving me control over how my copy and images fitted in as I went along, which is how I tend to work. Two important elements of the design process follow.

Cover Design

The cover is perhaps the most important element of your book, alongside the title, for the simple reason that it is what a potential reader will see first. You will be asked to approve the cover design, so make sure you express any concerns you may have.

Indexing

Depending on the type of book, an index may be required at the back of the book to help the reader find information with ease. Indexing is usually charged to the author, taken against any royalties due, but, if required, it is something that can be done by the author. Given the option, I chose to create my book's index and, once I worked out a rhythm, it was a straightforward process that took a couple of days to complete. Refer to Part Three: Finding A Good Editor – Indexing for a more detailed description of indexing.

Proofs

Proofs are the last opportunity to check and edit a book before it goes to print. A proof is a close representation of your printed book and you will need to go through and check that everything is as it should be. For example, all the images are in the right place, names have been spelt correctly, pages are numbered correctly, and so forth. A publisher will also use the proofs to check for things such as the colors reproducing correctly and the quality of the images. Proofs can be printed on several large sheets of paper, or supplied as a PDF. You will typically be supplied with one or two rounds of proofs; after that, any further changes you want will be charged per proof.

Sign-Off

Before your book is sent to print you will be asked to conduct a final review and sign-off the final proofs. Once this happens you can no longer change or correct anything.

Printing and Distribution

Once it is printed and packaged, your book is sent directly to the publisher's distribution service, and you will receive your agreed number of author copies.

Digital Books

A similar process to the one outlined above will apply. The difference is that you will approve artwork for the digital layout, and in place of print copies, will receive an agreed number of licenses to download the digital file.

What to Expect When Self-Publishing

As a self-publisher, you are responsible for the entire production process of your book. Be prepared for a steep learning curve with lots of trial and error, but, on the upside, you will gain plenty of valuable skills. The production process involves four key stages: editorial, design, print, and distribution.

Editorial

Manuscripts need to be edited. Editorial is where your manuscript goes through various rounds of editing to ensure it is in the best possible shape for publication. Editing is the process of checking and correcting spellings and grammar, as well as improving sentences, paragraphs and the overall structure of your book.

When you are in the writing stage, try to edit your manuscript as much as you can yourself in order to get it to a point where you feel that you can push it no further, much as you would when creating your content. Then turn to the professionals. Not getting your book professionally edited or having it badly done will harm your credibility, making you look both amateurish and cheap for not investing in the services of a good editor. **Hiring a good editor is an investment in perfecting the work you have done to write your manuscript**. There are several different types of editors, as follows:

- A **development editor** will pull your manuscript together, structuring the sections to flow cohesively and will advise on what to keep and what to get rid of

- An **editor** will improve your manuscript by checking the spelling, grammar, and punctuation; as well as checking the suitability of your manuscript for the intended audience, and suggesting word changes where appropriate

- A **copy editor** takes the work of an editor further by suggesting changes to enhance your book, helps simplify overly complex sentences, and ensures the consistency and flow of your manuscript

- A **proofreader** will check your manuscript for errors by comparing previous versions with the latest one to ensure all editorial changes have been implemented

- A **fact-checker** will verify the information included in your book, such as events, significant dates, quotes, names, captions, figures, tables, charts and so forth

It is not uncommon for some of the above to be combined into one editorial role.

Finding a Good Editor

The process is much the same as the one used to find a literary agent or publisher, so it's a combination of recommendations, search engine searches, and events. I have found my editors through networking events, the book industry professional services platform Reedsy, and the freelancer site PeoplePerHour.

Look for editors who specialize in your subject or category. Before you hire an editor, ask for work samples or view their portfolios to see who they have worked with. Even better, hire them to edit a few paragraphs of your manuscript for you to review and compare with other editors you are considering.

NOTE: Having more than one editor check your work to catch things that may have slipped through is a good idea, as it helps to ensure that your manuscript will be as good as it can be.

Other areas of the editorial process requiring specialist attention include:

Translation

If you intend to distribute your book in different countries or regions where your language is neither spoken nor read, your book will need to be translated. This requires the services of a translator with editorial skills.

Indexing

An index is the list of words and corresponding page numbers placed at the back of a book to help the reader find specific information quickly. It is especially useful for reference or text-heavy books, but not all books will need one. You can hire a freelance indexing specialist, but with a bit of organization and patience, you can do it yourself. Your book needs to have gone through the design formatting process, so that page numbers have been fixed in stone, for this to work.

First, scan through your copy to identify keywords that a reader is likely to search for, for example, cameras, equipment, lighting, styling, portraits, shutter speed, and digital formats would be relevant words for a photography book index. Put yourself in the shoes of the reader to gather all the words that are needed. Once you have your list, organize the words alphabetically, then open your design formatted manuscript, enable the software's finder or search box function, enter a word from your list and run a search, making a note of every page number it appears on. Repeat this process for all the words on your list. When this is completed, add the index to the back pages of your manuscript. Indexes can often run over several pages, as the more detailed your book, the longer the index tends to be.

That said, an index can be as short or as long as necessary. Remember to update it if you make changes to your information or page numbers.

Design

Once editing is complete, your manuscript will need to be formatted and packaged to suit the intended audience, which requires the services of:

A **designer:** to create the look and feel of your book, create the cover, and lay out the text and images, according to your book's specifications.

An **Illustrator:** to create specific graphics if required.

A **photographer:** coffee table books rely heavily on good professional photography as their primary selling point. The images you use will set the tone for your book, determining the overall visual aesthetic. Original photography offers exclusivity; however, as an alternative, you can source images from third parties, the drawback being no exclusivity. Free use of photography can be negotiated by getting the copyright holder to sign an image release permission form, granting the use of the images for your book and any related promotional activity. If you are commissioning images, bear in mind that in addition to a photographer a stylist may be required to set up the shots, which will impact your budget. Also, if your book gets published in several countries, you need to know if you would still have the rights to use the image or have to pay to use it with each edition. If so, rising costs could quickly cancel out any profit you were hoping to make. This is where contracts and licensing agreements are very important, even if you have been given permission to use an image free of charge.

Unless otherwise specified by your printer, images should be at least 300dpi in jpeg or TIFF file formats and, where possible, in the appropriate dimensions to suit your page size. This especially applies to your chosen cover image(s).

An **image editor**: Image editing is the quality control of any images that you use to ensure they are suitable for print. Where necessary, images are modified by retouching or color correcting to improve them. Some designers, photographers, and printers offer this service. If not, there are specialist image editing bureaus you can turn to.

Developers: to create e-books, digital books, and any apps required. You will need to make a note of the different e-book and digital book formats you want to distribute your book through, such as EPUB for Android, KF8 for Kindle, and enhanced digital books for iPad, to ensure that you select the right developer. The downside of hiring a developer is that you will have to pay each time you convert the file if you need to make changes to your book. So if you are willing to learn, you can create e-books and digital books yourself. Many platforms have step-by-step instructions to guide you through the process, and there is always YouTube.

If you are designing your book yourself and are using Adobe InDesign, the design industry standard, the software exports documents into EPUB format. In addition to this, many of the leading digital publishing platforms have created Adobe InDesign plugins that will help you with setting up files in the correct sizes to ensure you export your document to the right format.

If you do not have Adobe InDesign there are other options available for converting files into the required formats, such as Calibre software. If you are using Pages, the Apple Books for Authors software to create your e-book, you will need to reformat your book in another software, such as Adobe InDesign, to upload it onto other platforms, such as Kindle and Google Play Books.

Cover

Having spent months perfecting your book content, do not let a poor cover design ruin the effort. Your book cover is the first thing a reader sees, its purpose is to entice them into picking up your book. Your cover needs to stand out and command attention. Unless you are a designer, get a professional to design it, this is not the time to try it out for yourself!

However, not designing your cover does not mean you should have no input. Whilst it is good to have an idea of what you want when working with a designer, be open to their interpretations. Have a look at the covers of coffee table books that sell well. Do they have elements in common, if so what are they?

Take a look at book covers in your category, pay attention to the techniques used, ask your printer for options that suit your budget and feed this back to your designer. For my self-published books, I spent ages familiarizing myself with book cover styles and asking my printer questions.

Some authors have got their audiences and peers involved in their cover design selection process by posting cover mockups to get feedback. If you are not ready to share yet, maybe you could enlist the help of some people whose opinions you trust and respect to create your own closed feedback group.

When deciding on the final design, keep in mind where it will appear. When it comes to displaying online or on materials such as bookmarks, your cover must be able to scale down to thumbnail size without losing clarity.

Your cover should have:

Book Title: this includes the subtitle if you have one.

Author name: this includes co-authors or co-creators.

Blurb: a short piece of text, usually on the back cover to spark interest, which gives the reader an overview of what to expect inside your book. The blurb can be accompanied by complimentary quotes. Think of it as an elevator pitch, so you need to convey the key points in a few seconds.

Barcode: if you are planning on selling your book through retail stores, a barcode graphic displaying the ISBN details and the recommended retail price (optional) needs to go on the back cover. I explain the ISBN and its purpose in Part Three: What is an ISBN and Do You Need One?

Author photo (optional): this can go on the cover, on the inside flap, back page or inside back cover.

Publisher Logo (optional): if you have set up as an independent publisher, you can include your logo on the cover, front and spine.

Paper

If you are printing your book, the paper and cover it is printed on are both important. Paper is selected according to its weight and finish. The weight is the thickness of the paper, which is referred to as a number followed by gsm, e.g. 120gsm. The higher the number, the thicker the paper. Gsm stands for Grams per Square Meter.

The finish is how the paper looks and you can choose between coated and uncoated stock. Coated paper comes in a matte (subtle shine) or gloss (very shiny) finish. Uncoated paper has no finish and is rough-textured in appearance, an example being the paper used for a novel or workbook.

Your printer or print-on-demand service will advise you on suitable paper and provide samples for you to choose from. They can even create a digitally printed mockup of your coffee table book in your chosen paper, or a close match, before you commit to a full print run.

The paper weight you chose will dictate your printing options, as the heavier the weight, the more luxurious the feel, which means a higher cost too. Also, keep in mind that different printing processes handle certain weights.

Specialist finishes are available for your cover. Lamination in matte or gloss will help to protect your cover from wear due to handling. Varnish is another finish that comes in matte, gloss and spot UV. Spot UV is a high shine gloss that is applied to specific parts of your cover or the inside pages; for example, your cover could have a matte laminate finish with spot UV applied to the title lettering to make it pop.

NOTE: Applying varnish to your entire cover or whole pages is not recommended as it is prone to crack over time. Other finishes include metallic inks, as an alternative to spot UV, and laser cutting. You can also choose to have no finish, and leave your cover uncoated. Paper is not the only material for covers. You can choose from cloths, such as linen and silk, as well as rubber and even metal.

Having completed and edited your manuscript, designed your cover and formatted your book, the next task is to prepare your artwork for print or digital output.

Output

Before rushing off to the printers, you need to know how your coffee table book will be published and in what format. Questions you need to ask yourself include: are you bulk printing copies, going for print-on-demand, creating a digital book, or a combination of the different options?

There are three main output processes available to you:

- Traditional Print

- Print-on-Demand

- Digital Publishing

The chart below provides a comparison of using the different publishing options and their benefits.

TRADITIONAL PRINT	PRINT-ON-DEMAND	DIGITAL PUBLISHING
Emotive. This is more than just a book, it's a tactile object that engages all the senses and can be given as a gift or used as a decorative accessory to indicate status	Emotive. This is more than just a book, it's a tactile object that engages all the senses and can be given as a gift or used as a decorative accessory to indicate status	Practical. Quick access on a device wherever you are
Print book is a static object	Print book is a static object	Interactive e-books or apps can contain videos and sound, and links to relevant external information.
Not easy to update, requires new print run each time	Easier to update	Can be updated as and when required with current information
Non-reliant on energy to view	Non-reliant on energy to view	Energy required to operate the device
Booksellers take a percentage of each sale	Print-On Demand platforms take a percentage of each sale	E-book selling platforms take a percentage of each sale
Counterfeiting and piracy impacting sales	Counterfeiting and piracy impacting sales	Potential file security issues, and illegal digital file sharing
Shipping making storage a necessity, postage expensive or undeliverable to faraway places.	No need for storage. Platform prints and ships direct to customer	No waiting times to receive the book. The download is instant, which makes it easier to cross borders
More expensive to buy due to print costs	It depends on the platform's fees. A single copy can work out more expensive than a bulk print run	Low retail price

Higher print production costs = lower profit margins	Lower print production costs can = higher profit margins	Lower print production costs can = higher profit margins
Unsold copies remaindered, so sent back by sellers and destroyed or heavily discounted	No stock to hold, print a copy as and when required	Not a physical product
Can achieve a high-quality finish and photographic reproduction, particularly for artbooks	Digital print does not match the superior standards of litho printing when it comes to images	Works best for text-based books
Works best for long print runs, the more you print the cheaper it becomes per copy	Works well for short print runs	Unlimited copies

Let us look at each one in a bit more detail.

Printing

This encompasses traditional print and print-on-demand processes.

Traditional Print

In this day and age, one might wonder why anyone would bother with bulk printing copies of their book when print-on-demand and digital books offer a much cheaper and more practical alternative. There is no doubt that bulk printing books as a self-publisher can be very expensive, not to mention the cost of storing physical copies. No amount of mental preparation can prepare you for what 1,000 printed copies look like delivered to your doorstep. The sheer volume is huge and leaves you trying to figure out, what have I got myself into, and where am I going to store them?! So why would you consider this option?

It comes down to print quality and the type of book you are publishing. Coffee table books, as I previously highlighted, work best in printed form. This allows a reader to truly appreciate the presentation and quality in production, from the design and layout to the papers chosen. Printed books enable the reader to engage on a more personal level, and these often become collectables or cherished visual references that the reader refers to time and again for inspiration.

Traditional print refers to printing houses that use offset lithographic (litho) printing presses. This is a process that involves transferring wet ink onto rubber or metal plates that are then stamped on paper. Litho printing typically involves a four color process of Cyan, Yellow, Magenta, and Black (CMYK). So four plates are used to create a full-color image.

Additional plates can be used if your design requires a spot color. A spot color is a special ink, such as a metallic or a Pantone color, that cannot be achieved with the standard CMYK colors. **NOTE:** Spot colors will increase your print price because extra plates need to be used alongside the standard four plates. A Pantone color is a standardized numbered color matching system used across many industries. Litho printing allows for a paper weight of up to 500gsm.

Litho printing results in a smoother image when compared to the pixels (dots) visible with digital printing. This is the reason why litho is the best option for coffee table books that require superior image quality.

Understanding Image Quality and File Sizes for Print and Digital Use

To get the best out of litho printing high-resolution images are essential. Image quality is graded using a system known as dots per inch, commonly referred to as dpi. Dpi makes up the resolution, which is the level of detail contained within an image, and affects how it will reproduce when printed or displayed on a screen. The more dots per inch within an image the higher the resolution resulting in a sharp, crisp image. The fewer the dots per inch the lower the resolution resulting in a blurry, grainy image. 300dpi is the standard resolution for achieving high-quality printed images. While sufficient for print purposes, high-resolution images can slow down the processing of digital applications such as e-books and digital books. To overcome this low-resolution images at 72dpi are recommended for digital use.

Low-resolution images are commonly saved as jpeg or png file formats and typically have the kilobyte prefix, e.g. 60KB. High-resolution images are saved as jpeg or TIFF file formats and typically have the megabyte prefix, e.g. 25MB. Other file sizes are terabytes (TB) and gigabytes (GB) which result in massive file sizes, so unless you are saving complex images or creating videos, you would not need these sizes for your book. That said, depending on the total number of images you have in your book and their combined file size, your saved artwork for print or digital could end up as a gigabyte file size.

Litho printing is more cost-effective the more copies you print. 750 is typically the minimum amount a litho printing house will print. This is because the process involved in setting up the plates makes printing lower quantities unfeasible.

However, with the rise of the self-publisher, some printers have recognized a need for small quantity litho printing and now offer a short run service, but your price per copy will be high. Another reason litho printers have had to adapt is due to competition from the Far East, particularly China and Hong Kong, where a 750 minimum print run plus shipping costs can come in a lot cheaper than a local printer. That said, few printers from the Far East will consider a job of fewer than 10,000 copies.

Having considered my options and contacted a number of printers around the world for quotes, I decided that printing my self-published book locally in the UK, where I live, was my best and least expensive option without compromising on quality.

Another thing to consider when litho printing is the printing and delivery time that you will need to factor into your publish date. Litho printing can take around four to five weeks to deliver if you are printing locally. Make that a minimum of eight weeks if you are printing in the Far East, and factor in an additional two to four weeks if your print job falls during a festive period, like the Chinese New Year, as many factories close down for about two weeks.

Storage

Printed books have to be delivered to customers, but in the interim, they need to be kept in safe, dry, secure storage. Where you store them depends on the quantity and your circumstances, as they will take up valuable space in the home or studio. Having an empty waterproof garage or storeroom is a definite plus. If you have no space, an option is to work with a distribution company, who will hold the stock, handle inventory and deliver to the customer or retailer when needed. If your book sells well you can consider keeping the digital rights and assigning the printed rights to a publisher to handle on-going print runs and distribution.

Print-On-Demand

This is where technology meets print. Print-on-demand (POD) gives you the best of both worlds. If your book does not require the superior image quality of litho printing, then print-on-demand would be a suitable option. Print-on-demand relies on the digital printing process, which is much quicker than the traditional printing press.

Digital printing, like your home printer, relies on toners that spray dots of ink onto the page. Because the dots can sometimes be visible, the result is a less smooth image than litho printing. That said, advances in digital printing technology are bringing us closer to lithographic quality, making it almost impossible to tell the difference.

Digital printing also uses four color CMYK, but is different to litho printing because you cannot digitally print spot or special colors. However, because there is no printing press that needs to be set up with plates and ink, print-on-demand allows for a single copy or small quantities of a book to be printed as and when required.

This means there will be no bulk printing copies of your book, which does away with the associated upfront costs. Digital printing allows for a paper weight of up to 300gsm. Such is the improvement in the quality of print-on-demand, major publishers are using it to test out books and reduce storage, thereby reducing their costs.

Digital printing offers faster drying times so you can receive copies of your book within a couple of days of placing an order. This is why print-on-demand works so well for online platforms such as Amazon, which offers customers quick delivery services. Leading print-on-demand platforms include IngramSpark, Kindle Direct Publishing, Lulu, Blurb, Bookbaby, and Draft2Digital.

How to Find a Printer

Your book designer is a good place to start. Designers often have close relationships with printers. Again, ask for recommendations from your network and conduct an online search. Also, look at the copyright pages of professionally printed books. The printer's name and location are often included. I would suggest searching for and gathering a handful of names and contacting them directly for quotes and information such as turnaround times to help you decide.

When asking for a quote, include the following information (the printer or your designer can help you if you are unsure):

- **Binding**: the finish of your book, so hardback or paperback

- **Size:** the dimensions of your book, including the spine

- **Cover weight:** gsm, thickness of paper or other material

- **Cover paper/material:** type of material

- **Additional:** special finishes

- **Inside pages weight:** Paper's gsm

- **Inside pages coating:** Uncoated, coated, gloss, matte

- **Page count:** The number of pages

- **Quantity:** How many copies you want to order

- **Proofs:** PDF proof of physical mock-up

- **Delivery:** When you need your copies, and the delivery location

Digital Publishing

Both e-books and digital books are published in an electronic format for reading on digital devices, such as tablets, mobile phones, and desktop computers. As no physical product is published, they are the most cost-effective in terms of publishing options, not to mention the convenience they provide.

Available for instant download to your device at the click of the purchase button, e-books and digital books do away with delivery times and are highly accessible, especially if printed copies are expensive to purchase or ship to your own country.

E-books and digital books are published in several different formats, depending on the platforms you use to make your book available. The most common formats are PDF, EPUB, and KF8.

There is some debate over the terms e-books and digital books, as both are used interchangeably to refer to the same product. While an e-book is said to refer to PDF, EPUB, and KF8, a digital book refers to enhanced interactive books, audiobooks and book apps. This is an important distinction because when you get your ISBN and register your book, the system asks you to specify one or the other of the terms as the registered category. I will explain this in more detail in Part Four: Promotion – Metadata.

Digitally Publishing a Coffee Table Book

If coffee table books are meant for coffee tables, why then would you choose to publish a digital version?

Well, there are several reasons to consider this option. Firstly, a digital version would complement the printed version of your book, making the contents more widely accessible to audiences who don't have access to printed copies. Secondly, if your coffee table book is instructional, for example, flower arranging or sewing, a digital version of your book can enhance and bring the content to life.

Coffee table books are different from novels and solely text-based non-fiction books. They are aspirational and often seen as interior accessories; inspirational decorative details that are strategically placed on bookshelves, sideboards and coffee tables to be paged through at leisure. So the challenges of translating picture-heavy books onto the smaller digital screen has meant most coffee table books do remain in their print version only.

The desirability of a coffee table book lies in its subject matter and physical qualities. Due to their image-led aesthetic, coffee table books do not look great on black and white only devices. This means that not all coffee table books are suited to being published in a digital format. However, color screen digital devices provide good opportunities to take your book beyond the standard static images on a page by creating an enriching interactive experience with the addition of video, audio, music, slideshows, image galleries, and quizzes and games. Examples of this include AphroChic's *Remix* and Sabrina Ghayour's *Persiana* cookbook.

If you choose to publish a digital version of your book, you need to format it to suit the relevant digital formats, which could meaning making changes to the print version layout. Apple's Pages software enables you to create enhanced interactive digital books for iPad only. For other platforms, you can create an enhanced interactive digital book in app form by using software such as HTML5 and EPUB 4.

Platforms such as Instagram and Pinterest are good indicators of how your images will both look and be received digitally when you are deciding whether your coffee table book will work in a digital format.

Distribution

Distribution is the process of getting your coffee table book into the hands of readers. It is divided into:

Online

Printed copies are ordered at the reader's leisure, 24 hours a day, subject to their availability through your website, social channels, websites of booksellers, and other stockists. This is especially beneficial to readers who order from places where the books are not available to purchase locally, but can be delivered.

The advantage of e-books and digital books is that they enable customers to purchase and instantly download your book to their preferred device no matter where they are in the world, provided they have the necessary devices and access to technology such as broadband and Wi-Fi.

Offline

This relates to printed copies that are made available through traditional bookshops and specialist non-book related stores, including pet, DIY, and department stores, fashion boutiques, photographic, gardening, and home decor retailers, as well as trade shows and markets, conferences and talks, topic-related festivals and events such as food festivals for cookbooks and art fairs for artists. Other outlets include educational institutions, museums, galleries and libraries.

Some distribution channels are easier to set up or access than others, so unless you want to spend your time hauling books around market stalls and events, or become a Post Office regular, you may consider going through a formal distribution channel by working with a wholesaler or distributor. This a must if your goal is to get your book stocked in brick and mortar stores, especially the large chains, supermarkets, educational institutions and libraries.

The book-buying distribution channel is focused around central buying, which relies on book-buying chains. This means you cannot go direct to a bookstore chain, such as Waterstones or Barnes & Noble, to request they sell your book.

Wholesaler

Wholesalers are the middlemen between the publisher or author and a retailer. Book retailers order books from wholesalers. Wholesalers do not market or actively sell your book to retailers, rather the retailers come to the wholesaler.

The wholesaler functions as a central hub for thousands of books from publishers and authors, which makes it easier for a retailer to order the books they want in the quantities they need without having to negotiate with publishers or authors, which individually saves them a lot of time and effort. Ingram is the world's largest wholesaler. Others include Gardners, the UK's largest book wholesaler.

For a retailer to order your book from a wholesaler, they need to know about it and this is where a distributor comes in.

Distributor

A distributor helps to raise awareness of your book within the book-buying chain, makes the books it represents available to wholesalers and markets and pitches your book to retailers.

Wholesalers will typically require the publisher or author to have a minimum number of published books before working with them directly, whereas a distributor holds books from different publishers and authors so that it can meet the wholesaler's requirements.

In addition to this, good distributors will have established relationships throughout the book-buying channel to get your book in front of the decision-makers.

Distributors maintain exclusive lists and typically work with publishers and authors within specific niches and territories, as well as specific wholesalers. Territories is just another term for regions or countries. So, before you contact a distributor, make sure that your book is relevant and the distributor is connected to the bookstores you are targeting.

A distributor has a vested interest in promoting your book and can help boost your marketing efforts. For example, my distributor was instrumental in getting copies of my self-published book to an international event where I was speaking at short notice. This not only made my day when I saw them displayed by the venue entrance, but also meant I was able to reach a new audience.

Amazon is slightly different in that a publisher or author can have their books held directly through the commission-based FBA (Fulfillment by Amazon) service. This means that when a book is ordered on the platform, Amazon dispatches it, leaving you free to get on with your marketing or producing your next book.

There are dedicated distributor services for e-books, digital books, and print-on-demand. These include PublishDrive and IngramSpark, which, as a subsidiary, has access to the Ingram wholesale network.

Retailer

The retailer buys your book from the distributor to display in their stores for sale to their customers.

Wholesalers, distributors, and retailers do not charge upfront to distribute and sell your book, rather they earn a commission per sale. Commissions are said to range as follows:

Wholesalers/Agents: 50–55% of what they are offered by publishers.

Distribution: 66% of what they are offered by wholesalers.

Retailers: 40% of what they are offered by distributors.

As you can see from these figures, very little remains as a profit per book, not to mention author royalties.

Whether you choose to sell your book yourself, or work with a distributor to get your book into bookstores, retailers, educational institutions and libraries, you will need an ISBN.

What is an ISBN and Do You Need One?

What is an ISBN?

ISBN stands for International Standard Book Number. It is a globally recognized system for recording and keeping track of published books and other related media. You will be familiar with an ISBN as the string of 13 numbers that are usually included alongside the barcode on the back of printed books. **NOTE:** The ISBN is not a barcode, the barcode is a representation of the ISBN that a scanning device can read in order to find out the number. The ISBN is also included as a string of numbers on the copyright page at the front of your book.

An ISBN consists of five elements separated by dashes, as follows.

- The numbers 978 or 979, which tell us that it is a book

- A single number telling us the country or language of the book

- 3 numbers signifying the publisher

- 5 numbers that tell us the title, format, and edition

- A single number verifying the ISBN

Here is a breakdown of the ISBN assigned to this book:

Why is an ISBN Important?

If you want to get your coffee table book into physical stores, particularly the major chains, educational institutions, and libraries, then an ISBN is essential. This is because the serial numbers are used by book buyers, retailers, libraries, publishers, and readers to get information about your book. **Not having an ISBN makes it difficult to get your coffee table book stocked.**

Once an ISBN is assigned to your book you cannot use it for another book. This includes different formats of the same book. If you choose to publish your coffee table book as a hardcover, paperback, and e-book you will need a new ISBN for each. You will also need a new ISBN if you make significant updates to an existing book, as it will be seen as a new publication.

ISBNs can be purchased in most countries or territories from specialist agencies. To find your nearest one, use ISBN International: https://www.isbn-international.org.

The local supplier in the UK is Nielsen and in the US it is Bowker. Purchasing an ISBN works on the principle that the more you buy, the cheaper it becomes, and they are packaged accordingly.

The cost, at the time of publication, is:

1 = £89/US$125

10 = £164/US$295

100 = £369/US$575

Once you have purchased your ISBN you will also need to get it formatted by a separate agency into the barcode graphic to place on your book. The formatting costs range from free–£/USD$30. Some print-on-demand providers such as IngramSpark will format your ISBN within the cost of setting up your book's artwork for print.

Given the cost of a single ISBN, it can be tempting to take up the offers by some publishing services and platforms who will include one for 'free' or at a much lower cost as part of their service. There are also companies that produce barcodes, including ones for books, and offer individual ISBNs at a low price.

It is generally not a good idea to use these because the third group comprising three numbers that make up an ISBN, which signify the publisher, would be assigned to the service provider and not you. This can result in certain restrictions when it comes to having the correct metadata for book buyers, listing your book on other platforms, and negotiating rights. That said, if you don't intend to set-up as a publisher, or use your name as the publisher; and only intend to distribute your books via the global distribution service of a reputable print-on-demand platform such as Lulu, you can opt to use their free own-registered ISBNs.

Which brings us to the question...

Do You Need an ISBN?

Not every book will require an ISBN, it all depends on the goals you have for your book. If you plan to print a handful of copies to give away at an event, or only publish e-books, then you probably do not need one. If, however, you plan to produce a book series, set up a publishing imprint, or want your book to be stocked in as many bookstores as possible you will need one.

For books that do not have an ISBN, some platforms such as Kindle Direct Publishing will automatically issue their own book identification number. In this instance, it is a 10 digit ASIN (Amazon Standard Identification Number), which is not currently used by the wider industry.

The best time to get your ISBN, if you intend to use one, is whilst your manuscript is being edited and you are beginning your marketing efforts. It is worth noting that the key stages of the production process will overlap. So, to guide you, I have included a handy checklist in the resources section outlining when and where each stage typically occurs.

Barcodes

If your book is being printed and distributed and you have your ISBN, you will next need to generate a barcode and graphic incorporating your ISBN to place on the book cover. Barcodes are a unique identifier system made up of parallel lines and a string of numbers that machines can read. They are used to hold information about a product, in this case, your book. You can create a barcode using a free online barcode generator. If you are using a print-on-demand platform, some will generate your barcode as part of their service.

NOTE: If you are publishing your book with an ISBN in the UK, you or your publisher are required to send a copy to the British Library as soon as the publication date arrives. This is known as Legal Deposit.

Legal Deposit

The British Library has a system of collecting a copy of every book published in the UK. The system called legal deposit has existed in English law since 1662 and has enabled the Library to build up its vast resources. The system means your book can be read inside the British Library, as well as be preserved for future generations, meaning your book will become part of Britain's heritage. Print publications for legal deposit can be books or journals, magazines or maps, plans, charts or tables. Legal deposit has expanded to include digitally published material, such as websites, e-books, blogs, e-journals, and CD-ROMs. In addition to the British Library request, five other major UK libraries may also ask you for the print copy of your book. These are the Bodleian Libraries of the University of Oxford, Cambridge University Library, the National Library of Scotland, the Library of Trinity College, Dublin, and the National Library of Wales. If you are required to deposit an e-book, sending a copy to the British Library meets the requirements for all the other UK deposit libraries. You will normally receive a letter or email from the British Library requesting you to make your legal deposit.

The legal deposit system is not limited to the UK, many countries around the world have similar systems in place to collect copies of the books published within their borders. To find out the process for your country start by contacting your national library, a similar institution, or relevant governmental department.

Publishing Services

As a self-publisher going through the process of producing your first book, it is a challenging process that is, at times, frustrating and yet also highly rewarding. But if you do not want, or do not have the time, to go through the self-publishing process, you can opt for publishing services if you have the budget to do so.

Publishing services typically offer fixed fee packages that cover different aspects of the publishing process, for example, editing, formatting and design, and creating the e-book or digital book formats. But, as with vanity publishing, covered in Part Two: Planning Your Coffee Table Book – Vanity Publishing, the quality varies and you do not want to waste your money on a substandard end product.

I recommend caution and thoroughly researching your options before signing up to a publishing service. Have a look at their portfolio of work and the authors they work with, and read the reviews.

However you decide to produce your book, **you should not have to pay a publisher to publish your book**, as tempting as it may seem. By that, I mean signing a contract with an individual or a business to act as your publisher. This is because, more often than not, they do not take financial responsibility for the publishing requirements as genuine publishers do, and instead leave you with the bill by charging you for printing copies, offering 'guaranteed' promises that your book will be made available to, and stocked in, major retailers, and so forth. To use the cliché, if the offer sounds too good to be true, it probably is!

This brings us to the end of the publishing process. Although there is still a lot both to do and consider before you can get your book published, you will need to start thinking about marketing and promoting it.

PART FOUR

Promotion

Alongside developing your coffee table book, you also need to consider the activities of promoting and selling it. **Promotion is the process of creating awareness about your coffee table book so that you can sell copies. Promoting and selling your book is collectively known as marketing.** And with the online world teeming with endless do's and don'ts, this is a subject that warrants a book of its own!

The advantages of going with a traditional publisher are the contacts and allocated budget, albeit usually minuscule. A traditional publisher, however, will only allocate a set amount of time for promotion, usually two to three months. So, unless you are a big-name author, most authors find themselves shouldering much of the responsibility for promoting and marketing their book. So whether you publish traditionally or self-publish, getting clued up on marketing your coffee table book applies to you.

Rather than rehashing a list of standard marketing activities you can find on the internet, I shall instead zoom in on the specific book marketing-related areas of importance you may not be aware of that will help strengthen your overall book marketing strategy. This includes:

- Utilizing metadata and Search Engine Optimisation to increase the visibility of your book

- Crafting Advance Information Sheets and Press Releases

- Setting up a Press Kit

- Promoting your book to the press

- Getting yourself into the right frame of mind

Why is Promoting Your Coffee Table Book Important?

First off, your coffee table book is competing with thousands of others, and if no one knows about it, how can you sell it?

Awareness and sales come from people knowing who you are and what you do. As such, marketing also serves to get you, the person behind the book, noticed.

Whilst it can be tempting to keep knowledge of your coffee table book under wraps until the publishing date, promoting your book will typically start four to six months before launch. That said, with the publishing process continually speeding up, this time frame can be much shorter.

Waiting until your book is finished and published is one of the biggest mistakes authors make, especially first-time authors. This is something I am guilty of! When promoting my first book, I made so many mistakes, such as leaving the bulk of my pre-promotion to my publisher, not telling my blog readers about it until the launch date was upon me and more.

Truth be told, I was a) afraid of getting it wrong, and b) uncertain of exactly what I needed to do, despite having found the information that I needed to guide me. So I understand if you are not good at promotion, as it can be a daunting process, but with a bit of preparation and planning, you can create a promotional strategy that works for your book.

Planning Your Promotional Strategy

There is no one-size-fits-all when it comes to marketing your book. Your book marketing strategy will depend on whether it is fiction or non-fiction, and its niche.

Circling back to your market research, which I covered in Part Two: Doing Your Market Research, the knowledge you have gleaned about your target reader and the market itself will prove invaluable in steering your promotional efforts.

Your research will have given you an insight into the habits of your existing and potential audience(s). Don't forget to take into account the differences between online and offline reach, as they can vary in terms of the audience, communities, location, and so forth.

As a content creator, many of the marketing and PR skills you have picked up along the way will come in handy in promoting your coffee table book.

Your promotional strategy will be divided into three phases: pre-launch, peri-launch (middle of), and post-launch.

Pre-Launch

This is the preparation phase, when you plan out your strategy. If you haven't already done so, now is the time to register your ISBN. This means making the details of your forthcoming coffee table book available to book buyers and the trade.

The information contained in your ISBN is referred to as metadata, and you need to ensure it accurately reflects the who, what, why, when and where details of your book.

Metadata

Metadata is data about data. It is important because it is how your book will get found by distributors, wholesalers, bookstores, retailers, and readers. And with millions of books being published globally each year, the metadata (information) you provide will help them decide whether to stock it, buy it, and so forth.

We live in a data-driven world, with people entering keywords and phrases to find information that informs, entertains, educates, or inspires them. If you are a seasoned content creator you will be familiar with using metadata in the form of targeted keywords for your post headings, categories, tags, alt tags, images, captions, descriptions, hashtags, and so forth.

The aim of doing this is to get your content picked up by a viewer when they enter corresponding search terms and phrases into a search engine or search bar. Creating metadata for your book follows the same process of providing the necessary information that will help your book get found.

To illustrate the importance of metadata, a book of mine was on Amazon for nearly twice the price I had specified. As a result, it received a negative review based on the value for money (although the reviewer did say they liked the book and would buy it again if they found it cheaper elsewhere). I couldn't work out what the problem was until I contacted the Amazon support desk. It turns out that I had missed filling out a vital section of information (metadata) while listing my book, which fed into the system's auto calculations for pricing. This goes to show you how important it is to get metadata right, and how it affects sales.

The metadata for your book is entered and held in a central channel, such as Nielsens in the UK and Bowker in the US. These channels are linked to various book distributors, libraries, catalogs, and retailers. So any information you enter or change is fed out to wherever your book is listed.

Data drives publishing decisions, as decision-makers are constantly looking for information on what is new and popular, as well as the times spent reading and other reader habits to make sure they buy books that will sell. **NOTE:** If you are publishing your book traditionally, your publisher will fill out this metadata.

There are different kinds of metadata. For your book, you will primarily need the following:

- **Book title**

- **Author name**

- **Publishers name** (if setting up a publishing imprint)

- **Location**

- **Author bio**

- **Publish date**

- **Attributes:** Format (i.e. hardback, paperback), size, number of pages, images

- **ISBN**

- **BISAC Subject Codes:** e.g. photography, fashion, art, cookery, biography, historical

- **Target audience age**

- **Price**

Metadata does not end with information for your ISBN. You will also use it in the form of keyword-rich content anywhere you promote your coffee table book online, such as your website, blog, podcast, social media platforms, guest blogging, and videos to name a few. When planning your metadata you are essentially creating an SEO strategy for your book.

Search Engine Optimization (SEO)

Search Engine Optimization, otherwise known as SEO, has become increasingly important to digital marketing. In terms of promoting your coffee table book, it is one of the best ways to start spreading the word. SEO increases your book's visibility so that it ranks high in the search engine results, and thereby increases its chances of being found online.

Search Engines

Non-fiction books tend to be needs-based, read by people seeking a solution to a particular problem in their life, such as healthy eating, home decor inspiration, or learning how to publish a coffee table book! So one of the first places they look for information is search engines, where they type in the keywords and phrases that will lead them to the information they need and, in this case, your book.

There are several different types of search engines. Aside from the two most well-known, Google and Bing, did you know that Amazon, YouTube and, Pinterest are also considered search engines? At one point I didn't, but I do now! Knowing this will help you to fine-tune your SEO strategy for each platform you use.

Keywords

SEO is centered around keywords. These are words and phrases that best describe your book and will match what your audience is looking for. Seasoned content creators will know the importance of using keywords to help users find their content in search engines.

Finding the right keywords for your book is important because SEO will affect your search engine page ranking. In other words, how high up the list information about your book will appear in the generated results. You are aiming for the first page, ideally the top three results. This is because the majority of people rarely venture past the first page of results. When was the last time you did? You will also use your keywords in your promotional content and other marketing material.

It is essential that you continuously review your SEO strategy, tweaking your keywords until you get it right.

One overlooked SEO task is adding keywords to images and graphics. Many content creators neglect to name their images, simply defaulting to 13584.jpg, as labeled by their camera. Adding keyword-rich titles to any images and graphics you use will promote your book and also help it show up in a search engine's image search tab.

Other ways to boost your book's SEO strategy is by using keywords in video content and audio, and having a keyword-rich domain name/URL.

Video

Video trailers have become increasingly popular for both fiction and non-fiction books, as they can be shared on multiple channels. Videos with keyword-rich titles have a big impact on SEO results, as platforms such as Google, Bing, Facebook, Instagram, Pinterest, and TikTok continue to prioritise video-based content.

Audio

With the advent of voice-activated devices, audio is fast becoming another important marketing channel. Keywords in audio will need to reflect the natural human way of talking and asking questions.

Domain Name

Buying the domain name of your book title and creating a standalone website or platform for it can be a highly effective part of your book promotion strategy, particularly if the title is made up of keywords, or is a search term in itself.

The website can be a simple one-pager with all the relevant information. This works much the same way as having a landing page to promote a product or service, and gives you the option to drive interest directly to your book. You can then link the page back to your website, blog, social media platform or a retail site for purchasing.

TIP: Use Booklinker if you want to direct customers to a single Amazon link, instead of listing all the Amazon links for each of the different country sites where your book is available. This is a tool that creates one Amazon link for your book to direct readers in different countries to where they can buy your book on their local Amazon site.

Having mentioned websites and domain names, personal branding will have a role to play in promoting your coffee table book.

Your Author Profile

Your author profile falls into the realm of personal branding, and is the process of promoting yourself as the author of your book. Why is this necessary? Remember, promotion is also about getting noticed, because, as the saying goes, 'people buy people'.

At the end of the day, **your book is linked to you, the person, and the more people who are aware of you and come to trust you, the more likely they are to buy your book**. Even the most elusive or private of authors needs a personal profile, even if it is created around a pen name. Cultivating a personal profile is about giving your reader an insight into who you are and helping to build that all-important emotional connection.

Before publishing my first book, I didn't have much of a visible author profile, and I wish I had taken the time to properly invest in creating one. I hid behind my screen for a long time, but I soon realized that with my name as the author on the cover for all to see, I had to step out of my comfort zone and become more visible.

When I talk about building an author profile, I do not mean splashing yourself all over the place. It is up to you to decide how much of your life you want to share, where you want to share it, and with whom. **Building an author profile means taking a considered approach to how people will get to know more about you** and thereby your book. This, in turn, helps you to meet the objectives you set out in Part One: Why Turn Your Content into a Coffee Table Book? for publishing a book.

Author Page or Website

An author website or page is a central place to include information about you, and therefore plays a similar role to a standalone website for your book. Use an author page to link everything about you together.

If you haven't already done so, consider getting the domain of your name. Should you choose not to set up a personal website, you can always redirect the domain URL to the existing 'about me' page on your website or platform.

You can set up author pages on platforms such as Amazon and Goodreads, if you are promoting and selling your book through these platforms.

Amazon Author Page

If you are listing your book on Amazon, make use of the author page. You can add a bio, images, reviews, quotes, videos and other media, and link it to your blog, website, podcast, and social media platforms. This is great if your goal is to drive traffic to your website and let readers know about book signings or events. You can also, link any other Amazon listed books you have written, contributed to or listed as pre-sale.

The Amazon author page is a great tool that connects your personal brand to readers who are hesitant about purchasing your book and want to know a bit more about you. You do not have to be using Amazon's publishing tools to set up an Amazon Author page. To set up your page go to https://authorcentral.amazon.co.uk.

Goodreads Author Page

Owned by Amazon, Goodreads is a platform for readers to find, share, recommend and review books. For an author, Goodreads is a good place to promote your coffee table book, connect with your existing readers and introduce yourself to new ones. The types of marketing you can do here includes: polls, giveaways, Q&As and discussion sessions.

If you connect your blog to it, your followers will receive an email with your latest posts. To set up your page you will need to join the Goodreads Author Program: https://www.goodreads.com/author/program.

A key element of your pre-launch marketing stage will, of course, be letting the press know about your forthcoming book.

Promoting Your Book to the Press

The term 'press', used collectively, refers to journalists, editors, bloggers, podcasters, social media platform owners, radio and TV, amongst others.

Getting your book featured in magazines and newspapers, and on the websites, blogs, and platforms that are relevant to your topic will not only help expose your book to the right audiences, but can also boost your credibility as an expert in your field, if the publication or platform is prestigious, well-known and/or highly influential within your industry.

As you prepare to contact the press, it can be tempting to contact anyone and everyone with a popular blog, podcast, video channel or prestigious magazine, without giving a thought as to whether your book is right for them.

If finding the right press contacts proves challenging, you can use a specialist service such as whitefox or Reedsy, whose freelancers include experienced book marketing specialists.

Preparation for your press outreach will start by identifying the publications and platforms whose content is relevant to your book's subject area. You will go through a process that is similar to when you researched your book idea in Part Two: Doing Your Market Research.

To keep me on track, I find it handy to keep a spreadsheet of who to contact, when to do it, what the response was, the feedback, when to follow up, and so forth.

When contacting the press about your book there are several things to include:

- An advance information sheet

- An offer of a review copy

- A press release

Advance Information Sheet

Four to six months ahead of publication, traditional publishers send out what is called an Advance Information sheet (AI). The purpose is to inform the press and retailers about the forthcoming publication of a book which they feel would be of interest to them.

Think of the AI as a save the date notification. Should your press contact be interested in the book, the AI gives them time to prepare and schedule in their reviews. This is especially important for print-based publications which tend to work to strict long-lead deadlines, typically four to five months in advance. As a guide, short-lead journalists, bloggers, and content creators work only one to four weeks in advance.

If you are self-publishing you can still send out an AI.

The AI format is a simple one-pager that summarizes the key information and metadata about your coffee table book. So the title, author's name, publisher's name, book specs: page count, price, images, publication date, a brief description of the book, a thumbnail image of the book cover, and contact details to find out more. The document can be in black and white or full color. The AI can be a Word document, a PDF, or a link to a webpage. Illustration 1.1 shows what an AI can look like.

Once you've sent your AI, those interested will usually let you know when they will need the information and a review copy.

Review Copies

To review your book, journalists and other press contacts will often want to see a copy of it, whether it be in print or digital. This is known as a review copy. **Review copies are given to reviewers before the book is available for sale.** That said, once your book is published you can and will receive review copy requests, particularly in the weeks following publication.

Review copies are not just for journalists and the trade. If you have been involving your audience in your book production journey, offering select readers a review copy in exchange for a Wordery, Amazon or other online book retailer review can help drive interest in your book.

A word of advice when it comes to giving out review copies: you need to be selective with who you give them to. This is because you are giving away a free copy of your book, which costs you money to produce and print. So you need to be savvy about genuine reviewers versus those looking for a freebie. The review copies are accompanied by your official press release.

Inspiring Books Press

Illustration 1.1.

ADVANCE INFORMATION

All information is provisional and subject to change.

A STYLISH HOME: INSPIRATION FOR STYLING YOUR FIRST HOME

Voysey Tan with a Foreword by Taylor Jones

Moving into your first home is such a special time filled with thoughts on how to put your stamp on your new space. Interior decorator and stylist Voysey Tan shows you how to create a stylish home. She guides you through choosing investment pieces that will be with you for years to come and how to use accessories to a character.

Voysey's hands-on exercises will have you bringing your ideas to life and creating a space you can truly call home.

Provisional Publication Date: January 2020

KEY SALES INFORMATION

- Guides the reader through the basic principles of interior design
- Multiple hand-on exercises such as creating moodboards
- Includes example interiors and how to get the look
- Bursting with stylish full colour images of interior inspiration
- Includes a directory of retailers and resources

Extent: 144pp

Size: 21 x 21 cm

Binding: Hardback

Approx. 200 colour illustrations

Price: £12.99

ISBN: 978 0 98765432 0 1

CONTENTS

Foreword; Introduction; Interior Decorating Basics; Finding Your Interior Style; Working With Colour Palettes; Selecting Statement Pieces; Choosing Accessories; Home Inspiration; Glossary; Directory; Image Credits

AUTHOR

Voysey Tan is a London based interior decorator and stylist. With an eye for bagging the best bargains Voysey is known for creating stylish looks on a budget. Her work has appeared in high-profile publications, among them *Luxury Living*, *New Home*, and *Interior Style*. Voysey is a judge on TV1's *Interior Style Challenge with Taylor Jones*. *A Stylish Home* is her first book.

INSPIRING BOOKS PRESS
123 Paperback Lane
Binding, W1 ACB

t: +44 (0)20 1234 5678
t: +44 (0)20 1234 5690

e: pr@inspiringbookspress.com | w: www.inspiringbookspress.com

Press Release

You will begin sending out your review copies and your press release from three months before publication onwards. Your press release will contain similar information to your AI. So the title, author's name, publisher's name, author bio, book specs: page count, price, images, publication date, a summary and description of the book, a thumbnail image of the book cover, and contact details to find out more. While the press release can also be a Word document, PDF, or a link to a webpage, journalists are said to prefer the press release's content to be pasted directly into the email message. Illustration 1.2 shows an example of a publisher's formatted PDF press release.

Having sent out the AI and then the press release, you will most likely receive requests for web or print-ready images of the cover. If a review happens to be a substantial feature, there may be a request for images of the inside pages, additional information about both the author and the inspiration behind the book, or even a request for an interview.

Preparing for these requests ahead of time will enable you to respond with the required material quickly. This calls for a press kit.

Press Kit

A press kit is one of the most useful tools to have in your book launch marketing strategy. It is **a collection of relevant information about your book, all stored in one place**.

A press kit is typically presented either as a document with several pages (usually saved as a Word document or PDF), or as several files saved in a digital folder that can simply be stored as a zip file on your desktop or device, in Cloud storage, or in an open or password-protected area on your website, ready for when you need it.

Inspiring
Books Press

Illustration 1.2.

PRESS RELEASE
for immediate release

Publication Date: 1st January 2020

Extent: 128pp
Size: 14.85 x 21.0 cm
Binding: Hardback
Approx. 120 colour illustrations

Price: £9.99

ISBN: 978 0 12345678 0 9

Available to purchase from all good bookstores

NATURE UP CLOSE:
A PHOTOGRAPHIC ESSAY
Dixon Banks

Nature as you have never seen it before.

Discover a world of enchanting nature. Photographer Dixon Banks takes you into the heart of nature at it's best and harshest moments. From icicle-covered caves to the first shoots of spring meadows *Nature Up Close* will transport you with its breathtaking imagery, making you rethink how you view and interact with our amazing world. Discover a world of enchanting nature.

Photographer Dixon Banks takes you into the heart of nature at it's best and harshest moments. From icicle-covered caves to the first shoots of spring meadows *Nature Up Close* will transport you with its breathtaking imagery, making you rethink how you view and interact with our amazing world.

From icicle-covered caves to the first shoots of spring meadows *Nature Up Close* will transport you with its breathtaking imagery, making you rethink how you view and interact with our amazing world. Discover a world of enchanting nature. Photographer Dixon Banks takes you into the heart of nature at it's best and harshest moments.

Dixon Bank's invites you to discover a world of enchanting nature. Photographer Dixon Banks takes you into the heart of nature at it's best and harshest moments. From icicle-covered caves to the first shoots of spring meadows *Nature Up Close* will transport you with its breathtaking imagery, making you rethink how you view and interact with our amazing world.

AUTHOR
Dixon Banks is a Dorset based photographer and television presenter. Her award-winning nature photography has appeared in high-profile publications, among them National Geographic, Wildlife Now, and Amazing Planet. *Nature Up Close* is her third book.

MEDIA REQUESTS TO:
INSPIRING BOOKS PRESS

e: pr@inspiringbookspress.com
w: www.inspiringbookspress.com

e: pr@inspiringbookspress.com | w: www.inspiringbookspress.com

This is especially important if you receive an urgent request for information while on the go, but a press kit will also save you time, as you will not have to scramble around for information each time a journalist or editor wants additional information or images from you. Before I created press kits for my books, I would find myself going through the same steps of gathering everything together, recreating bio content, figuring out what to say, and trying to email big files. It was a messy way of working!

Having everything organized in a press kit helps to avoid the errors and inconsistent messaging that can occur if you keep having to find information or create content each time you get a press request. **A press kit also gives you some control over how you share various elements of your book and your story**.

What to put in your press kit

Your press kit will contain the following key information:

- Your **author bio**

- An **author image** saved in both low and high resolution files sizes for digital and print use. It is a good idea to have both black and white and full-color versions

- **Press releases or news** about the book, for example, a press release to give to the press if your book wins an award

- An **image of the book jacket**, both front and back cover, saved for digital and print

- A **selection of official press images** these could be of the interior pages and images used in the book

When you have created your press kit, keep the link or folder where you can access it if you are away from your computer, laptop or device. And remember to keep your press kit up-to-date.

This brings us to the end of the pre-launch planning stage. There is a lot to consider so you can see why it needs to begin four to six months before your book's publishing date.

Peri-Launch

The peri-launch is the phase where your coffee table book has just launched and is now available to buy. This phase of your marketing activity focuses on the weeks in and around your book's publication date and builds on what you have put in place in the pre-launch stage. This period can last anywhere from two weeks to three months, depending on your or your publisher's budget.

You are looking to maximize the attention you began generating for your book in the pre-launch phase to drive greater awareness, reviews and ultimately sales. The peri-launch is the time when all those reviews and interviews you lined up will be released or take place. The peri-launch phase is also where book launch parties and book tours happen.

Book Launch Events

Book launch events are a time to celebrate your achievement of writing and publishing your coffee table book, generate buzz and, of course, sales. Once a standard in the publishing industry, traditional publishers tend to keep the book launch party or tour for well-known, big-name authors, as marketing budgets have dwindled.

So, if you are planning on the traditional publishing route and want to have an event, you will need to organize and fund it yourself. The same goes for self-publishers.

Having an event to launch your coffee table book is a great way to meet and interact with your online community offline, strengthening those all-important connections. It enables you to offer what cannot be replicated online. So if a physical event is something you want to do, don't let the expense put you off. Instead, look for solutions to make it happen. For example, get sponsorship for a venue, partner with your local independent bookstore who may host the event, or combine your book launch with a workshop related to your book topic, such as silk fabric painting techniques if your book is about silk fabric painting, and create a ticketed event around that. The possibilities are there.

Virtual Events

Another alternative to a physical book launch is a virtual event, which requires little to no monetary investment. Many authors are opting for online versions of a book tour in the form of readings or Q&As hosted on platforms such as YouTube Live, Facebook Live, Instagram Stories, Twitter, Goodreads and the #BookTok communities on TikTok to connect with their audiences and spread the word about their book.

Post-Launch

Once the flurry and excitement of your coffee table book launch has died down, you will start settling into your long-term marketing strategy. This phase can last as long as your book is in print or available for sale. In other words, promoting your book is a continuous process.

Cultivate a good relationship with your distributor if you are working with one. Your distributor's marketing efforts can complement your own and vice versa. I am always looking for ways to link retail and trade buyers to my distributor for my self-published books, and to my publisher for my traditionally published book.

Publish your next book. Successful authors recommend publishing more than one book. Doing so increases your credibility and awareness of your name, helps drives traffic to books you have already published, and you can use these books to drive sales by up-selling or cross-selling.

Up-selling is the process of getting a customer to buy a complementary, higher-priced product; for example, if you publish a book on organizing your time, you may also offer a luxury journal that complements the book. **Cross-selling** is getting your customers to buy a similarly priced complementary product. So, for example, if you were publishing a series of travel-related coffee table books, a reader of one book will be more inclined to buy the other books in the series.

Get back to doing what you do best. Keep creating quality content. After spending all that time planning and producing your coffee table book, the last thing you probably want to think about is consistently producing content. I get it, I have been there. But the content you have been creating is what led to you self-publish a coffee table book, or what attracted a traditional publisher to your work in the first place. And your content is what is going to keep you relevant, build your audience, and drive traffic towards your book.

Working With a Publicist

If you don't want to manage your marketing or need some help to enhance your strategy and you have the budget for it, consider working with a publicist. A publicist's role is to generate and manage publicity for your book. A traditional publisher will assign a publicist to market your book, and they will inform you of the marketing plan. To complement their own contacts, they will ask you, as the expert in your field, for your input with regard to relevant publications, platforms, and contacts that they should approach to review and write about your book. This helps to ensure your coffee table book is brought to the attention of the relevant people who may not be on the publisher's radar.

If you are self-publishing, you can hire a freelance publicist. Publicist services range from simply writing your press release to managing your entire marketing strategy. As such, the more they do for you the more it will cost you. Again, finding a publicist will be a similar process to finding an agent or a publisher. Platforms such as Reedsy and Bibliocrunch offer industry professionals who have been vetted.

Some Other Things You May Want to Think About

Bestseller Lists

Some authors deliberately target and make a big deal about bestseller list status as part of their marketing strategy. This is because of the belief that appearing on bestseller lists can lead to a dramatic increase in sales.

Bestseller list status can bestow an element of prestige upon you and your book. Not to mention the fact that getting to the top of a category list on a platform like Amazon means that your book will most likely come up first in related on-platform keyword searches and algorithm recommendations, helping it to stand out from the crowd.

Promotion

But getting onto a bestseller list isn't as simple as selling enough books to qualify, which typically means shifting anywhere between 3,000–10,000 copies in the first week of publication. There is more to it than that.

Bestseller lists work by calculating the sales of books by booksellers and retailers in a given period. However, not every store or retailer selling books is considered. Those that make the selection, usually a small selection, are chosen by the owner of the list. This opens the selection process up to biases based on what those booksellers involved feel are worthy of inclusion.

There are a number of bestseller lists, the most well-known perhaps being Amazon Lists, and the most prestigious being The New York Times Bestseller List. But, given how bestseller lists are compiled, there are increasing questions over their relevance amid controversies over how the lists are compiled, and who is compiling them.

If you are considering targeting bestseller lists as part of your strategy, you would be wise to first concentrate your efforts on marketing your book to your audiences and engaging with them to get the sales. Then, if you do achieve bestseller status in the process, think of it as a bonus.

Setting Online Alerts for Your Book

Set up Google Alerts for your book title. That way you can monitor any mentions and link to them in your press and news pages. To set up alerts, follow the link to access the alert page: https://www.google.com/alerts, add your book title or topic, then hit the create alert button. You can set up as many alerts as you like. Once they are set up you will start receiving email notifications every time your book is mentioned. You can change the frequency of the notifications to suit you.

Having Books for Events

Capitalize on any events you get invited to as a speaker, panel guest or workshop host by taking along a stack of books. If you are traditionally publishing your coffee table book, or if copies are being stored by a distributor, make sure you keep some copies to hand in case you need some at short notice. Alternatively, if there is enough time, you can put your publisher or distributor in touch with the organizers to get copies delivered. This has been very helpful for me when I have had international speaking engagements that require copies of my books, as it means I don't have to lug heavy books through the airport.

Book Fairs

Book fairs are where the business of books happens. They are the marketplaces where publishers present their titles and where rights negotiation, sales, and distribution deals take place. Book fairs tend to be professional B2B industry-related events and are not typically open to the public.

Publishers and other related industry suppliers, such as printers and distributors, will use book fairs to boost brand awareness and generate new business. Although selected authors may be invited to speak, book fairs are not usually the place for authors to promote themselves. Indeed, for an individual author or a small independent publisher on a budget, exhibiting at a book fair is often out of reach due to the high costs involved.

For an author, book fairs are good places to learn about the industry, discover new trends, meet other self-publishers and authors, attend the author seminars and workshops, meet publishers, get advice and speak directly with suppliers, like printers. You can ask them questions, view their portfolio of books to gauge the quality, and even get event discounts. However, do keep your wits about you, as vanity press type publishers love to frequent these events in order to entice would-be authors with too-good-to-be-true deals.

Awards

Awards and prizes can bring attention, publicity, prize money, and increased sales. However, it has been said that winning an award does not always translate into an increase in sales. That said, winning an award for your book can bring you both exposure and attention in your industry, which is particularly useful if attracting speaking engagements is one of your goals. And, on a personal note, winning an award for your efforts is just nice.

To find awards that you can enter in your country, region or industry, as well as globally, carry out a search using a variety of keyword phrases, such as 'non-fiction lifestyle book awards' or 'coffee table book awards', then follow the guidelines to submit your application.

Bear in mind that awards where you have to submit will often charge entry fees and require you to send in a copy of your book. Also keep in mind that if you get shortlisted, it may mean having to buy tickets or a table to attend the award ceremony, and incurring other related costs, such as a new outfit, travel and accommodation. This means that entering an award can end up costing you more than you make back in sales.

This brings us to the end of Promotion. Whatever shape your book marketing strategy takes, remember the golden rule – always keep your reader at the center of your efforts.

Last Word

Publishing your book is all about perseverance, getting organized and staying the course. The biggest lesson I have learnt from my book publishing experiences is that you have the choice to publish your book in a way that suits you and your circumstances.

Traditional publishing is often pitched against self-publishing, and printing against digital. Do not think of it as a conflict between them, where you have to stick to one or the other. We are lucky to be publishing at a time where **we have options to choose a production and publishing process that suits each of our different books**.

It is no longer unusual for an author to self-publish a series of novels, yet seek out a traditional publisher for their coffee table book; or choose to have a digital download and audio version of their printed book.

Going with what works for your book will help increase your chances of success, and many successful authors do that to reach as wide an audience as possible.

So there you have it, a practical guide on how to publish a coffee table book. I hope you have found the information and tips useful and look forward to hearing how you get on.

And I wish you the very best of luck!

Resources

References

A list of the links and resources mentioned throughout the book

Flood, A. 2014. https://www.theguardian.com/books/2015/mar/24/jk-rowling-tells-fans-twitter-loads-rejections-before-harry-potter-success. The Guardian Online.

Loum-Martin, Meryanne. 2021. Instagram post @meryanneinspired. https://www.instagram.com/p/COQjAlohkZb/?igshid=YmMyMTA2M2Y=

Wyatt, D. 2014. https://www.independent.co.uk/arts-entertainment/books/news/zoella-zoe-suggs-book-girl-online-becomes-biggest-selling-debut-novel-ever-9898676.html. Independent Online.

Guinevere. 2012. https://storify.com/chroniclebooks/from-blog-to-book-alt-summit-2012. Chronicle Books.

Newport, C. Deepwork. 2016. https://www.calnewport.com/books/deep-work/. Paitkus.

Einlyng, P. 2016. http://www.sweetpaulmag.com/crafts/a-talk-with-grace-bonney. Sweet Paul Magazine.

Ahern, A. https://abigailahern.com/blogs/abigail-aherns-blog/behind-the-scenes-writing-a-book/

Coveteur. 2016. https://coveteur.com/2016/10/03/how-to-publish-coffee-table-book/

Waterstones - https://www.waterstones.com

Barnes & Noble - https://www.barnesandnoble.com

Amazon - https://www.amazon.com

BBC. 2019. https://www.bbc.co.uk/programmes/m0007syq. The One Show.

London Book Fair - https://www.londonbookfair.co.uk

Ingram Spark royalty calculator - https://myaccount.ingramspark.com/Portal/Tools/PubCompCalculator

2019. https://www.britishprint.com/industry-news/more/28625/the-resurgence-of-print-books/. Two Sides.

Penguin Random House - https://www.penguinrandomhouse.com

Hachette - https://www.hachette.com/

HarperCollins - https://www.harpercollins.com

Simon & Schuster - https://simonandschusterpublishing.com/

Pan Macmillan - https://www.panmacmillan.com

Pearson - https://www.pearson.com/uk/

Oxford University Press - https://global.oup.com/?cc=gb

John Wiley and Sons - https://www.wiley.com/en-gb

Black Dog Publishing - https://www.blackdogonline.com

Jacqui Small - https://www.quartoknows.com/imprints/1026/Jacqui-Small/

Apple's iBooks Author - https://www.apple.com/uk/ibooks-author/

Milliot, J. 2018. https://www.publishersweekly.com/pw/by-topic/digital/content-and-e-books/article/76706-e-book-sales-fell-10-in-2017.html. Publishers Weekly.

Thames & Hudson - https://thamesandhudson.com

Phaidon - https://uk.phaidon.com

Taschen - https://www.taschen.com/

Prestel - https://prestelpublishing.randomhouse.de/PublishingHouse/Prestel/58500.rhd

Rizzoli - https://www.rizzolilibri.it

Chronicle Books - https://www.chroniclebooks.com/

Art/Books - https://www.artbookspublishing.co.uk/

Abrams Books - https://www.abramsbooks.com/

Artisan Books - https://www.artisanbooks.com/

Assouline - https://eu.assouline.com

Rocket 88 - https://www.rocket88books.com/

Essential Works - https://www.essentialworks.co.uk/

Hoxton Mini Press - https://www.hoxtonminipress.com/

Creative Market - https://creativemarket.com

The Society of Authors - https://www.societyofauthors.org

Alliance of Independent Authors (ALLI) UK - https://www.allianceindependentauthors.org

The Authors Guild - https://www.authorsguild.org

Kindle - https://kdp.amazon.com/en_US/

Google Play Books - https://play.google.com/store/

Remix: Decorating with Culture, Objects, and Soul - https://books.apple.com/us/book/remix/id650565085

Persiana - https://books.apple.com/gb/book/persiana/id940046907

Booklinker - https://www.booklinker.net

Goodreads - https://www.goodreads.com

Amazon Author page - https://authorcentral.amazon.co.uk

Goodreads Author Program - https://www.goodreads.com/author/program

Pew Centre - https://www.pewresearch.org/fact-tank/2022/01/06/three-in-ten-americans-now-read-e-books/

Image Credits

Cover, p10, 14, 17, 28, 80, 114 evermotion, PixelSquid

Book Interior Front Matter Pages Examples p41 Mockups Design

Book Cover Layout Example p92 Pavel Danilyuk, Pexels; MockUp Template TinyDesignr

Advance Information Sheet Example p129 kaboompics_Cabinet_with_gold_decorations_and_eucalyptus

Press Release Example p131 kaboompics_Ficus_Lyrata_Leaf.jpg

Book Production and Publishing Process Checklist

These are the key steps identified in the book writing, production, publishing and distribution process. Update to suit your needs.

1. Select a topic and research suitability, potential audience interest, and estimated costs to produce.

2. Develop the concept further, decide key book specifications, size, number of pages, and images whether color or black and white or both, word count, sections, design, print options, and the delivery deadline for manuscript and artwork if required.

3. Write book.

4. Take or source photography. Where applicable the author to ensure image release permission form signed.

5. Look into distributors.

6. Look into licensing and international rights agreements.

7. Purchase ISBN numbers for each book and obtain barcodes.

8. Set up template of book.

9. Design cover and other elements such as a book jacket.

10. Get quotes for hardcopy or digital printing specifications.

11. Marketing and selling of the book begins.

12. Prepare Advance information sheet.

13. Manuscript reviewed by copy editor, images reviewed for quality.

14. Review and approve edits, manuscript proofread.

15. Layout and design of book, images selected and typesetting and formatting of the text.

16. Selected images sent to reprographics.

17. Final document edits and proofreading.

18. First round of printers proofs including cover.

19. Corrections made, where necessary.

20. Final printers proofs in PDF, author signs of for print. Any changes to be made at this stage incur charges.

21. If being printed artwork is sent to print.

22. If digital e-book created.

23. Printed hardcopy proof received to check quality.

24. Book printed, receive advance copies.

25. Send requested review copies to magazines, journalists, blogs.

26. Printed copies delivered or sent directly to distribution or storage centre.

27. Book officially published or uploaded, now available to purchase.

28. PR and marketing continues.

Publishing Toolkit

A handy list of information and links for helpful tools and resources to produce and publish your book.

TRANSCRIBING SPEECH TO TEXT

Descript – https://www.descript.com

Gboard – virtual keyboard app developed by Google that does Voice Typing

Just Press Record – https://www.openplanetsoftware.com/just-press-record/

Otter – https://otter.ai

Speechnotes – https://speechnotes.co

EDITING

Bibliocrunch – https://bibliocrunch.com

PeoplePerHour – https://www.peopleperhour.com

Proof Reading Pal – http://proofreadingpal.com/

PTC Publishing Training Centre – https://www.publishingtrainingcentre.co.uk/freelance-finder

Reedsy – https://reedsy.com

Society for Editors and Proofreaders (SfEP) – https://www.sfep.org.uk/directory

whitefox – https://www.wearewhitefox.com

TRANSLATION

Speak Thy Language – https://www.speakthylanguage.com

EDITING APPS

Grammarly – https://www.grammarly.com

Hemingway – http://www.hemingwayapp.com

ProWritingAid – https://prowritingaid.com

DESIGN PROFESSIONALS

99designs – https://99designs.co.uk

Behance – https://www.behance.net

Bibliocrunch – https://bibliocrunch.com

Creativepool – https://creativepool.com/

Dribbble – https://dribbble.com

Fiverr – https://www.fiverr.com/

PeoplePerHour – https://www.peopleperhour.com

Reedsy – https://reedsy.com

ebook launch – https://ebooklaunch.com/

Upwork – https://www.upwork.com/

whitefox – https://www.wearewhitefox.com

DESIGN/LAYOUT APPS/ SOFTWARE

Adobe InDesign - https://www.adobe.com/uk/products/indesign.html

Canva - https://www.canva.com

Adobe Express - https://www.adobe.com/express/

Marq - https://www.marq.com/

Pressbooks - https://pressbooks.com/self-publishers/

PRINTERS (LITHO)

Biddles - https://www.biddles.co.uk/book-printing/

Couture Book - https://couturebook.com/

KOPA - http://www.kopa.eu/

Orphans press - https://orphans.co.uk

Print Ninja - https://printninja.com

PRINT-ON-DEMAND

Blurb - https://www.blurb.co.uk

Bookbaby - https://www.bookbaby.com

Draft2Digital - https://www.draft2digital.com

IngramSpark - https://www.ingramspark.com

Kindle Direct Publishing - https://kdp.amazon.com/

Lulu - https://www.lulu.com

WORKFLOW

Agenda - https://agenda.com

Bear - https://bear.app (for iOS devices)

Evernote - https://evernote.com

PUBLISHING SERVICES

whitefox - https://www.wearewhitefox.com

WHOLESALERS

Amazon - https://www.amazon.com

Gardners - https://www.gardners.com

Ingram - https://www.ingramcontent.com/

DISTRIBUTORS

Bookbaby - https://www.bookbaby.com

IngramSpark - https://www.ingramspark.com

PublishDrive - https://www.publishdrive.com

RIGHTS

PubMatch - https://www.pubmatch.com

ISBN AGENCY

The International ISBN Agency - https://www.isbn-international.org

Nielsen - https://www.nielsenisbnstore.com

Bowker - http://www.bowker.com/products/ISBN-US.html

BARCODE SUPPLIERS

International Barcodes - https://internationalbarcodes.com

Buy Barcodes - https://buybarcodes.co.uk

CROWDFUNDING YOUR BOOK

Kickstarter - https://www.kickstarter.com/

Unbound - https://unbound.com/

PROMOTION

BookBub - https://www.bookbub.com/users/sign_in

NetGalley - https://www.netgalley.com

PublishingPush - https://publishingpush.com

MARKETING/PUBLICISTS

Bibliocrunch - https://bibliocrunch.com

Reedsy - https://reedsy.com

whitefox - https://www.wearewhitefox.com

For a printable version of the Book Production and Publishing Process Checklist and a clickable version of the Publishing Toolkit visit: https://www.tapiwamatsinde.com/how-to-publish-a-coffee-table-book/and follow the instructions to download the files. You will need the password: HTPACTBSP22.

CPSIA information can be obtained
at www.ICGtesting.com
Printed in the USA
BVHW061017231222
654916BV00023B/949

9 780995 470682